"Kathleen Chapman, writing in a very conversational, practical, and often humorous style, had me in her introduction! She delightfully points out that worship for children is not singing 'God Is So Good' fourteen times . . . but rather helping children discover a million fascinating things about an awesome God. And she is convincing that this discovery will glue a child to God . . . forever. If you're a parent . . . you'll be encouraged. If you're a grandparent, your heart will be awakened to a whole new purpose in life! If you're a children's pastor . . . you'll recognize this familiar topic but discover some fresh new dimensions. If you're staff on the children's ministry team in your church . . . help is on its way! If you're a seminary professor, you might be disappointed. If you're a seminary professor *who has young children,* you will love it. If you're a typical worship leader . . . beware!"

—Dan Johnson, the Idea Agency

"*Teaching Kids Authentic Worship* is a valuable and timeless book. Children who are taught real worship at an early age have learned to profess the truth about God. That's powerful since so many misunderstandings about both ourselves and about God originate in childhood. Buy this book to teach the children you love, and its truths will affect your own worship as well."

—Rich Buhler, speaker, author, broadcaster,
creator of TruthOrFiction.com

"Kathleen Chapman is the most creative person I know. She literally has helped thousands of children (and adults too!) enjoy and experience a more vibrant faith in God through creative worship experiences. This book is practical, hands on, experiential, and life-changing."

—Jim Burns, president, YouthBuilders

"Kathleen Chapman has written the definitive book on teaching kids the purpose, meaning, and way of worship. Period. Kathleen's passion for God and for kids explodes out of her writing. Crack open page one and your view of worship will never be the same. Not only is the book required reading for parents, Sunday school teachers, and worship leaders, this book takes the reader past mere information to the heart of spiritual transformation. A lifelong practitioner of worship, Kathleen writes with depth, humor, insight, knowledge, and experience for what it takes to glue a kid to God. Filled with practical ideas, this book will challenge you and inspire you personally and professionally. It's so sticky you won't be able to put it down."

—Joey O'Connor, author of the So What?! series for teens

"In business, rule #1 is 'Keep the main thing the main thing.' Kathleen sets forth a guide for parents and all those who work with children to help them not only understand what worshipping God is, but how to do it. As parents and teachers, our God-given responsibility is to train and prepare our children for a life that honors God. In the life of a child this is the main thing."

—Gary B. Dixon, chairman of the Northwest Christian Education Conference, consultant for Cook Communications Ministries

"I don't know anyone on the planet more enthusiastic about children or more passionate about creatively teaching them to love and worship God with all their heart, mind, soul, and strength than Kathleen Chapman. Her new book aims not only to shape a whole generation of authentic young worshippers, but also the church they inhabit and the world they in turn will seek to impact and influence for Jesus Christ."

—Denny Bellesi, senior pastor, Coast Hills Community Church

"There's no doubt that Kathleen Chapman has a unique ability to connect with children and lead them to God. Now she shares her unique, compelling, and colorful methods with parents, teachers, and church leaders. Let God use these pages to guide you in pointing children to a lifelong relationship with God through worship. This book represents an investment in eternity!"

—Mary Hunt, founder and editor of *Cheapskate Monthly*

"Kathleen has captured the essence of teaching children to worship."

—Johanna Townsend, president, For Kids Only,
Newport Beach, California

"Once again I find myself learning from Kathleen! This book will not only help you to teach kids more about worship—it will teach you how to develop and deepen your own worship of God too."

—Tom De Vries, director of church multiplication and revitalization,
Reformed Church in America

"Well, here it is. The search is over for the ultimate guide to teaching kids authentic worship. God has blessed Kathleen Chapman with gifts in challenging and motivating children that I have yet to see matched. Her experiences are documented brilliantly to make this book a treasure for children's ministry programs and families around the world. Now, this is worship!"

—Dean-o Lies, leader of Dean-o and the Dynamos,
Mission Viejo, California

TEACHING KIDS
AUTHENTIC
WORSHIP

How to Keep Them Close to God for Life

KATHLEEN CHAPMAN

Baker Books

A Division of Baker Book House Co
Grand Rapids, Michigan 49516

© 2003 by Kathleen Chapman

Published by Baker Books
a division of Baker Book House Company
P.O. Box 6287, Grand Rapids, MI 49516-6287
www.bakerbooks.com

Third printing, January 2005

Printed in the United States of America

Library of Congress Cataloging-in-Publication Data
Chapman, Kathleen, 1946–
    Teaching kids authentic worship : how to keep them close to God for life / Kathleeen Chapman.
        p.   cm.
    Includes bibliographical references.
    ISBN 0-8010-9153-5 (pbk.)
    1. Worship (Religious education) 2. Church work with children. I. Title.
BV1522.C457 2003
248.3—dc21
                                                2003001865

For the lights and loves of my life,
Nancy, Mark, and John

And the loves of their lives,
Bob, Anne, and Heather

And
for
Sophie

CONTENTS

ACKNOWLEDGMENTS

My thanks and appreciation to:

My husband, Duane, for partnering with me these thirty-three years, growing our three kids to know God. I love you forever.

My sister, Susan Anderson, for your brain, for pushing me to places I never dreamed attainable, and for your four precious boys, whom I've questioned to exhaustion over their lifetimes.

Jannet Kunkel, my oldest friend and cohort in life. Your love for kids and encouragement in ministry have spurred me on many times when I wanted to quit.

Mary Hunt for your friendship, unmatched wisdom, and brilliant advice about writing a book.

Joyce Dalby, who makes me laugh in the twinkling of an eye; Bonnie Fevergeon, who lets me dream as big as the sky; Tom Devartanian, who uses the biggest words I've ever heard in my life; and all three of you for your remarkable editing skills.

Johanna Townsend for unparalleled passion for children's ministry and for making much of the research needed for this book possible.

My support teams in every church where I've ministered. This wouldn't have happened without you.

The thousands of kids these past three decades who taught me how to teach kids the importance of worshiping God.

My mom and dad, Burt and Velma Clements, for making loving God nonnegotiable in our house.

INTRODUCTION

I grew up in church and still love God. I am one of the survivors. Many are not so fortunate.

Why? What's wrong? What's missing? How can kids walk away from what has been part of their lives for years and not look back?

In my thirty years working in children's ministries, I've seen virtually every gimmick used to keep kids interested in church—cutting-edge marketing tactics, high-tech worship, and low-pressure religious strategies. Yet these ploys haven't made much impact; kids continue to walk away from God. No matter what the church affiliation, economic situation, or ethnicity, the exodus continues.

More than twelve years ago, I resolved to find a *glue* to stick kids to Christ, uninterrupted for life. It had to be strong enough to withstand the unpredictable journey through the teen, college, and adult years. It had to be guaranteed to adhere through feast, famine, or unbelievable pain—a sort of spiritual Super Glue!

I was motivated to begin this quest because I passionately love kids and work with them every day. Children deserve the opportunity to know Christ and His protective, unconditional love as they embark on this earthly venture called life. It is eternally lethal to entertain the idea that children can go it alone. A heart without God is doomed. A life without God is tragically empty and potentially devastating.

My search resulted in a mind-blowing discovery, shaking me to the very core of my Christian life and ministry. The answer was always there, though for so long I failed to recognize it.

The glue is *worship*—worshiping God!

Wait! I don't mean "worship as usual" as you or I may have experienced. I have reached some shocking conclusions about what I now know to be authentic biblical worship. In fact, I'm more convinced than ever that *worship* is the most misunderstood and misused word in the religious world.

Practicing authentic biblical worship as God intended produces supernatural adhesive. Simply put, an authentic biblical worship relationship with God generates glue so strong nothing on earth will break its hold. If children are worshiping God the way God intended and Scripture instructs, they don't walk away from Him.

Knowing this truth is only the first step. If true worship is not *taught,* it will never happen. My prayer is that by the time you finish these first nine chapters, you will know how to teach children the truth about worshiping God, thus gluing them to Him for life. I pray that by chapter 10 you'll be eager to begin this process today.

Twelve years ago I emerged from a lifelong spiritual coma into a life of biblical worship. Today more than ever, I am determined to shout about this glue from the housetops.

You *can* keep your kids glued to God!

I was raised in a Christian home, committing my life to Jesus Christ as a six-year-old. I casually sauntered with Him into adulthood—a Christian and churchgoer—remarkably, never walking away.

Without realizing what was missing, I limped along in my relationship with God. Yes, it is possible to be a veteran believer and never truly worship God!

Accepting Jesus as the Son of God and giving your life to Him is only the first step. This gets you into heaven. This is not worship.

The word *worship* is overused, misused, and sometimes abused. It needs to be explained anew—especially to children and to those who teach them.

Here is a simple assignment: On a piece of paper, write *your* definition of *worship*. In a sentence or two, describe what you think it means to worship God. Now fold the paper and place it at the end of this book. Go ahead. I'll wait. Please do this before you read another word. Don't look at your description again until you finish the book.

All done? Good! I already love you for your desire to read on this subject. We have volumes in common if there are children in your life in need of the glue and you care enough to do something about it.

Let's go!

IN SEARCH OF THE GLUE

There is no new thing under the sun.

Ecclesiastes 1:9 KJV

When I began my search, I never considered worship a viable candidate for the glue. It wasn't even in the running. I desperately searched for why and how children could easily lose interest in the things of God, especially if they had been committed to Him at one point in time.

Church kids all across this country are walking away from church and God every day. George Barna of the California-based Barna Research Group notes that his organization's research "has consistently shown that between the ages of 18 and 24 we lose a very large percentage of young people who had been regulars at church."[1] Barna has also stated that "the next wave of adolescents will baffle their elders by happily embracing conflicting beliefs and values, and unorthodox views about God."[2]

Regrettably, kids who have grown up sitting in weekly church classes, memorizing Scripture verses, and winning prizes at Vacation Bible School are turning their backs on God. I have helplessly watched as many of my children's friends left the faith and kids I

17

Dear God,

You made the stars and the sky. You love SOOOO big, and you don't get mad easy. You made cats, dogs, parrots, and people.

Love, Sarah P., age 7

had worked with disappeared, leaving me wondering what happened.

The exodus seems to rear its ugly head sometime after sixth grade. It's a subtle transformation in some cases. Middle school students inconspicuously begin to drag their feet about attending church. High school kids lose interest in church as school studies and social functions create busy schedules. Many college-age young people convince themselves that their agendas don't leave time for church, or so they claim.

God is quietly transferred to the proverbial back burner. Why is this happening? What can reverse this epidemic and stick kids to God for life?

As I watched kids I knew head into a mire of godless existence, my search for the glue took on an urgency unlike anything I had felt before. I wasn't sure where to start, but focus groups sounded feasible. As I traveled the country, teaching seminars to children's ministry leaders, I was able to question hundreds of kids, teens, and adults.

I also asked my own three teens and their friends questions like, Will you continue to attend church and walk with God in your future? Why or why not?

Many couldn't answer these simple questions. Many answered honestly that they couldn't promise anything. Others reserved the right to make the decision when the time came. Others glibly answered, "Hey, what's with the guilt trip?"

What an eye-opener! Very few were excited about the things of God.

I hadn't found the glue, but knew I was on the right track.

About this time, I received an invitation to train ministry leaders on how to lead children in worship. Of course, I foolishly believed my qualifications fit the criteria: I had taught Sunday school forever, never missed church, attended Christian schools, married a wonderful Christian man, and introduced my own three children to Jesus. In addition, I am a musical theater veteran. I've led kids in worship most of my life. No problem! This would be easy.

Our beliefs on any given subject are like tapes playing in our heads. These tapes have been accumulated from what we've heard or been taught during our lifetimes. Only when we deliberately choose to learn more about something can these tapes be interrupted or corrected.

Well, one of the tapes playing in my head was, "When you are in church, especially when you are singing in church, you are worshiping." So I figured I'd teach on inspired singing of some sort. Maybe, though, I should do some research—just in case worship included something else.

I checked the newly revised edition of *Webster's Dictionary.* Under *worship* it said, "See adoration." *Adoration* means "deep, ardent, often excessive attachment, passion, love."

"Excessive attachment, passion"? No mention of singing.

Anxiously I scoured religious books and magazines. I wanted to use some big words so I'd sound credible. I read everything I could unearth on worship.

Interestingly enough, some rather curious definitions emerged: Worship is "one dimensional." Worship of God is "God-centeredness" (a nice big word).

I called my brother, Gary (a senior pastor), who upon hearing my dilemma, smiled over the phone. (I could sense it.) He suggested researching worship in the original languages of Scripture (what a concept!)—what worship means, how it originated, why God demands it, and when and how and why we are to do it as believers.

I found thicker books with bigger words. Although I was initially terrified, I explored Hebrew and Greek definitions of *worship.* Thus far in my research, I found that the word *worship* only spoke of God's worth and our responsibility to adore Him. It wasn't about music or singing, and it wasn't about me.

Wait a minute. It wasn't about *me?* I needed to look further.

What about kids' worship? After all, that was my real interest. I visited Christian bookstores and contacted a dozen publishers.

Dear God,

*You are everything
that is wonderful.
You are more perfect
than perfect. You love
everyone and You are
really so special. You are
everywhere. You made
everything, and You are
the one and only God. You
are the One I will follow
my whole entire life.*

Love, Michelle W., age 10

Lucky for me!—worship for kids was a hot topic.

There were worship lesson plans and curricula from various denominations, worship games, and crafts . . . but oddly enough, I couldn't find the actual definition of *worship* in any of them.

My curiosity was piqued. Was there anything that taught the *what* of worship so children could better understand *how* to worship? If the *what* of worship was not in the curriculum, then did kids know what the Bible says about it or how to do it?

My next step: more focus groups. Polling hundreds of kids would produce more accurate data than someone's personal theory or opinion. What did kids understand about worship?

First, I questioned our church kids and pulled together teams from other churches to question their kids. For months the teams questioned almost every child they saw. Passing out questionnaires in churches, malls, parks, and various neighborhoods, we asked the following questions:

1. What is worship?
2. How do you worship God?
3. Why do you worship God?
4. When do you worship God?

The first five hundred answers left us numb and disheartened. Most kids didn't know the answers to basic questions about worship or God!

I was stunned. Maybe the fault was in the questionnaire. Maybe we had slipped up somewhere in our survey.

We decided to try again, asking children one-on-one, "Would you tell me all you know about God and worshiping Him?"

When the answers remained vague at best, my serious side emerged full throttle. I got on my knees. *Lord, help! What is going on? How can five hundred kids not be able to explain the meaning of worshiping You?* (Even worse, the teachers we questioned couldn't explain it either.)

Why was I surprised? What had I known about worship as a child? What did I really know now?

I was one of the privileged. I grew up in a wonderful Christian home. Our family went to church religiously. It was never multiple choice (Honey, would you like to go to church today, or would you rather play sports or go out with your friends?). If the church doors were open, we were there.

My brother, sister, and I committed our lives to Jesus at a young age. When I was a child, summer church camps resulted in "mountain-top" experiences, leaving me euphoric for weeks at a time. Teen retreats gave me warm fuzzies, and visiting evangelists spurred me on with more ministry energy. As an adult, I was busy teaching Sunday school, working on committees, and devoting many hours to service in the church. I was quite pleased with my commitment to God.

Looking back, I had equated all these wonderful feelings with worship. Regretfully, most of it had been about me, what I enjoyed doing. However, the definitions of *worship* I had gathered so far had nothing to do with *me*.

My research revealed that worship is more than singing or going through some weekly church ritual. Worship is more than completing a page in a church lesson book or reading prayers aloud in a church service. Worship is more than faithful service. It's more than reading your Bible or having a mountain-top experience at a retreat.

Dear God,

You made dolphins, bunnies, and flowers. You love everybody. Thank you for making Noah in the Bible.

Love, Kaeli B., age 6 1/2

Worship is more than loving God.

That's right. It's *more* than loving God. Slowly the fog began to lift. This was big. My explanation of worship was rapidly changing, and drastically so!

Worship isn't about me at all.

A. W. Tozer said, "Worship is to express in some appropriate manner a humbling but delightful sense of admiring awe and astonished wonder and overpowering love in the presence of . . . our Father which art in heaven."[3]

Not about me.

So the questions hit home: Have I ever worshiped God? Have our kids ever worshiped God? Have the kids in our churches ever really worshiped God? If not, what will happen once we understand and begin truly worshiping God the way He intends?

Learning these earth-shattering truths changed my world! And, wonder of wonders, could this revelation have something to do with the missing glue?

Absolutely!

The glue is not church attendance. It is not Bible study, not a prayer meeting, not music or singing, not memorizing verses, not tithing, and not faithful service. It is not baptism and not some mysterious theology or ritual connected to any particular denomination or religion.

The glue is not simply loving God.

The glue is *worshiping* God.

I had finished leading a seminar in Texas on teaching kids about worship when a very distraught woman approached me.

"My seventeen-year-old son and fourteen-year-old daughter have been worshiping in church their entire lives." With tears streaming down her face, she continued, "They still go, unwillingly, because it's a rule in our home that we all worship as a family. Last week our son told us how much he hates going to church, and his younger sister, who idolizes him completely, agrees with him. They won't even close their eyes during prayer anymore. They want nothing to do with church or God, and it's breaking our hearts. What happened?"

Knowing a verbal answer wasn't appropriate just then, I put my arms around her and prayed. How many times have I heard this in the last twelve years? "Worshiping" their entire lives? Obviously, something hadn't stuck with her two kids either.

I find the same scenario everywhere I go. My desk is cluttered with letters from parents crying for help. The stories are endless, the pain unfathomable.

Our friends have two beautiful, intelligent kids, both raised in a solid Christian church and home. Sadly, their son has decided that God no longer fits into his lifestyle. Consequently, he has dropped out of high school, has chosen injurious habits and friends, now has a police record, and still believes he can make it without God.

> Dear God,
>
> Thank you for writing stuff down to help everyone. No matter what people do, you want them closer to you. You show Your love through Your awesome creation.
>
> Love, Brian P.,
> age 13

Kids need our help! We can't *guess* what goes on inside children's minds. We don't know which ones aren't sticking . . . until it's too late. There must be more we can do while they are still in our care to ensure that their hearts are affixed solidly to God.

A number of years ago, on my way to a play rehearsal, I received news that one of the fourth-grade students in the play had attempted suicide. We used the rehearsal time to pray for the child, but we were all in shock. Weeks later we were told the child believed there was no one who wanted her to live. She wasn't from a Christian home but faithfully attended our weekly kids' choir program. We only had one hour each week to show her how much God loves her—an hour a week to make the glue available to her. We missed the mark.

According to the Academy of Child and Adolescent Psychiatry, suicide is the third leading cause of death for fifteen- to twenty-four-year-olds and the sixth leading cause of death for five- to fourteen-year-olds.[4]

Read that paragraph again. These are the demographics in your community and mine!

Young children can experience pain and emptiness powerful enough to convince them no one cares.

There is an urgency today, like never before, to glue children to the God of the universe. God loves them far more than they can imagine, and He will ease their pain and fill their emptiness with hope. This loving God desires a lifelong relationship with every single human He creates.

Several months after beginning this search, not only did I find the glue, but I also felt like a newborn Christian in many ways. I experienced a renewed awe of God, an unparalleled passion to know Him better. I discovered a newfound truth—I began worshiping God.

Today I know beyond any shadow of doubt that we parents, grandparents, aunts and uncles, teachers, and believers need to first get *our* acts together. We need to understand and experience true worship ourselves before we can teach this truth to children.

The true definition of *worship* has nothing to do with denomination or specific church preference. It doesn't stipulate that you stand with arms raised or kneel on a prayer bench. It doesn't discriminate about the day or time. Most important, the age of the worshiper is inconsequential.

God simply demands and expects worship.

> Ascribe to the LORD, O families of nations,
>   ascribe to the LORD glory and strength,
>   ascribe to the LORD the glory due his name.
> Bring an offering and come before him;
>   worship the LORD in the splendor of his holiness.
> Tremble before him, all the earth!
>   The world is firmly established; it cannot be moved.
> Let the heavens rejoice, let the earth be glad;
>   let them say among the nations, "The LORD reigns!"
>
> 1 Chronicles 16:28–31

PART 1

WHAT

WORSHIP

The Definition

The LORD spake, saying, . . . I will be glorified [worshiped].

Leviticus 10:3 KJV

God asks us to respond to who He is through worship. It is only by God's grace that we can dare to come into His presence in the first place.

The act of worshiping God is not new. It has been around since Adam. The idea of kids worshiping God is not new either. It's been around since Abel.

Worship is a lovely, religious-sounding word. Most people, whether they have ever attended church or not, are at least familiar with the idea of worship. Almost every denomination in the world uses the word *worship* in some form of liturgy. In fact, that is part of the problem.

Most church-going adults believe they have experienced worship. They presume it has been happening throughout their entire lives. I did. After all, the bulletin says "worship service," doesn't it? As a matter of fact, most people who don't regularly attend church still assume they have participated in some form of spiritual worship during their lifetimes.

Don't take my word for it. Spend a day randomly asking friends, family members, coworkers, and even perfect strangers if they have ever worshiped God. (Of course, be prepared for some strange looks!) People tend to think having attended one church service means they have worshiped God. (I had a couple of people ask if attending funeral services counted!)

While waiting for a delayed flight at Chicago's O'Hare Airport, I randomly asked fellow passengers, "Would you mind telling me if you worship God or how you feel about it?"

Here are some of the responses:

"Me, worship God? I don't know, probably."

"Worship depends if you are a spiritual person or not; I'm not."

"No. I'm not a religious person."

"Worship is something private. You can worship without believing in any particular God."

"Do you mean church? I'm not sure what you mean by worshiping God."

"Sure, doesn't everybody?"

"I'm not sure. I think sometimes. Why do you want to know?" (I had a nice chat with this young woman.)

"No." (I got a lot of these.)

"That's a weird question." (I got a lot of these.)

"Of course. Everybody can worship by simply watching a beautiful sunset. It feels so wonderful."

"Sure, I go to church."

Guess what! Church attendance doesn't equal worship! Watching a sunset doesn't equal worship any more than a lot of other things we've been doing.

Twelve years ago I didn't know the definition of *worship*. The word *worship* translates "God's worth." The act of worship is focusing on Almighty God and Him alone. It's the act of assigning to God His true worth.

"Worship," according to Marva J. Dawn, "is derived from an old English root word meaning 'worth' or 'worthiness.'"[1] It's *singular*—the word was used to indicate the worth of a notable person.

Dawn goes on to say, "We devise ways to honor God that bespeak his worthiness, all the while recognizing that our attempts are inadequate."[2]

> Dear God,
>
> You are awesome. You are the only one worth living for. You know all and are in control of everything. Your love has no conditions and it never changes. You are the Rock of the world and the Foundation for all.
>
> Love, Danny P., age 16

This may not sound extraordinary at first, but worship can only be about one subject, and it's one-sided. Therefore, as I refer to worship, please note that I'm not talking about church or a music service.

The Hebrew word *shakhah* means "to prostrate oneself, to bow in homage, to do reverence." This is the most common Hebrew word translated "worship" in the Old Testament. It represents an acknowledgment of who God is—His attributes, person, and character.

The Greek word *proskyneo* means "to worship, to do obedience, to do reverence." This Greek word is found fifty-nine times in the New Testament and is used exclusively for the worship of God or Christ.[3]

In both cases, worship pays deference to God alone.

My dad was the first person ever to say, "There is nothing new under the sun, so it's what you *do* with things that makes the difference." (At least, he *told* me he was the first person ever to say it!)

So if there is nothing new under the sun, what cutting-edge, revolutionary approach do I have to this age-old word (or tradi-

> Dear God,
>
> You are hard to imagine, but the Bible says you are really true. You are very amazing because of everything you've made. Thanks for the ocean. (It's my favorite part.)
>
> Brad J., age 10

tion)? How could it possibly change the course of this world for children, and even adults, who want the truth about worship today?

Well, I'm thrilled you asked, because I'd love to tell you.

Worship is about God. It has nothing to do with you or me. It's only about God. The truth is, it's not about us at all. I am fiercely emphatic about this definition because we're talking about *children* understanding worship.

The explanation must be clear so they grasp the truth. Our postmodern world indoctrinates children into believing everything is about them. Worship is one of the few things where the focus is completely off of them. Worshiping God is focusing only on God.

Kent Hughes, senior pastor at College Church in Wheaton, Illinois, says, "The unspoken, but increasingly common assumption of today's Christendom is that worship is primarily for us—to meet our needs. Such worship services are entertainment-focused, and the worshipers are uncommitted spectators who silently grade the performance. . . . Taken to the nth degree, this instills a tragic self-centeredness."[4]

Ours is a self-absorbed age, and the church has followed suit. True worship is rare! According to George Barna, "Many adults find that having a truly worshipful experience is not something they can turn on and turn off at will. . . . Having never been taught much about worship, they find the inability to interact with God on a deeper level frustrating, but don't know what to do about it."[5]

Our children especially don't get it! My fourth- and fifth-graders wrote letters to God one Sunday during class. My instructions were to address their letters to God and write *only* about God—everything wonderful about *Him*—not mentioning themselves so we could call them *worship* letters.

The first ten started out similarly—"Dear God, I love You so much." Telling God how much you love Him is not worship. It's wonderful. It's your adoration. But it involves you. True worship is adoring God *alone* without ever mentioning yourself.

It went downhill from there. Not one of the letters just adored God. They were full of lists of stuff God had given them and done for them!

They didn't get it. Why should they when for years I didn't get it either?

Worship is one-directional. Worship is focusing on God and giving all glory to Him only, alone, singularly, totally—just Him. If this still doesn't sound world shattering, just keep reading.

According to Jack Taylor's *The Hallelujah Factor,* a Hebrew word for worship, *barak* (used repeatedly in the Old Testament), means "to pay singular tribute to *God alone.*"[6] This one word is used more than seventy times to denote blessings to God alone. Taylor cites the following examples:

> The LORD gave and the LORD has taken away;
>   may the name of the LORD be praised *[barak].*
>
> Job 1:21

> Wherefore David blessed *[barak]* the LORD before all the congregation.
>
> 1 Chronicles 29:10 KJV

There are many other words in Scripture that do the same. For example, *khavah,* meaning "worship, kneel, prostrate," is mentioned sixty-five times in the Old Testament.[7]

Some Greek words in the New Testament that literally mean "worship"—God's worth—may be translated either "praise" or "glorify." However, in these cases they always pay singular honor to God alone! For example, *doxa* (noun) and *doxazo* (verb) can be translated "glory" and "to glorify." Taylor cites Luke 2:14 as an example: "Glory *[doxa]* to God in the highest and on earth peace to men on whom his favor rests."[8]

There are hundreds of other examples, but this chapter is not intended to be a study in Greek and Hebrew. But these word studies emphasize an important point: Worship is not about us but about God and God alone. Let this phrase sink in for a moment. Worship is all about focusing on God. Period.

One day I was driving nine-year-old Jenna home from our musical theater rehearsal. I asked her to define a few religious terms for me—*salvation, repentance, forgiveness*—and she easily answered. Then I said, "What about *worship?*" She was quiet for a few minutes and then said, "Do you mean church?"

"No," I said, reemphasizing the word *worship*.

My young friend was silent again before hesitantly answering, "I don't really know."

"Worship is only about God," I said.

Then I gave her a simple definition, explaining that it's like a "you are" prayer to God and that she should do this without mentioning herself. I told her to tell God some things she loves about Him without using any personal pronouns.

Searching for words, she finally said, "I don't think it's easy to pray without mentioning myself."

Dear God,

You are so wonderful. You are mighty and very powerful. Your love is greater than anything and anyone's love for each other. You forgive no matter how much people sin against You or others. You forgive and forget. Your mercy is too much to put into words. You are so strong. You can overthrow death. You are the most divine Being to ever set foot on this Earth.

Yours forever,
Jenna Lynn W., age 10

That's exactly the answer I hear all the time—maybe not the exact wording but the same conclusion. And it's not coming only from children.

God created worship for Himself alone. Included may be elements of praise, tribute, thankfulness for who He is, adulation, adoration, devotion, love, and anything that is *only* about God. Psalm 29:2 says, "Worship the LORD in the splendor of his holiness."

Worship has nothing to do with me or what God has done for me or how I feel! I never knew this truth as a child. Obviously, I didn't know it most of my adult life. I never taught it to my own three kids. Much of what the church practices as worship is not even close to what God spells out in Scripture!

Singing isn't worship unless the song is about God alone. How many of the songs we sing and call worship are all about us? Read the words to the onslaught of new choruses and see how many pay homage to God alone. It's a chilling reality that most of our time before God is spent focused on *us*.

Lessons, crafts, Scripture reading, dramas, busywork, service—none of this is worship unless all we see is *Him*. It must point to *Him*, adore *Him*, and bring glory to *Him*.

The things listed above are actually *our* praise, *our* thanksgiving, *our* love for him. Yes, God certainly appreciates these things and desires them, but they aren't worship. Praise, thanksgiving, and love may be the direct result of a worshipful life, but they are not worship.

I was amused to hear of a friend's visit to an Easter service at another church. She said every song was about *us!* She counted the pronoun *I* twenty-eight times in one of the songs that morning. The sermon was about what Easter does for *us*.

They weren't worship songs. It wasn't a worship service, even though the bulletin said it was. We can love God, be enormously grateful to Him for all He has done for us, and talk to Him all the time about how much He means to us. However, this is not worship. Worship speaks only of God.

This is serious. This is His instruction. Psalm 45:11 reads, "Because He is your Lord, worship Him" (NKJV). When God gives instructions, he obviously wants them followed.

Cain learned this lesson the hard way. He decided to worship God the way *he* wanted by presenting an offering of *his* choice rather than doing what God had told him to do. A curse was later put on him (see Gen. 4:11).

King Herod was smitten with worms and died when he refused to give praise (singular honor—*doxa*) to God alone (see Acts 12:23).

Please don't misinterpret what I'm saying. Yes, we are to praise God! Yes, we are to thank Him for everything He has done for us. Yes, we are to ask Him about every part of our lives. But we must not confuse praising God with worshiping God. There is a difference. Praise is about *us*—our response to what God has done for *us*. Worship is about God—all adoration, adulation, awe, devotion, homage, honor, reverence, and wonder for who God is and what He has done.

Worship comes first. It is, by direct order from God, the most important thing a Christian is to do. First Samuel 15: 24–31 records the story of how Saul repented of his sin and knew his first move was to worship God. Psalm 22:27 says, "All the ends of the earth will remember and turn to the LORD, and all the families of the nations will worship before Thee" (NASB). The implication is that worship comes *first*, before doing anything else.

Psalm 96 reads,

> Sing to the LORD a new song;
> Sing to the LORD, all the earth.
> Sing to the LORD, bless His name;
> Proclaim good tidings of His salvation from day to day.
> Tell of His glory among the nations,
> His wonderful deeds among all the peoples.
> For great is the LORD, and greatly to be praised. . . .
> But the LORD made the heavens.
> Splendor and majesty are before Him,
> Strength and beauty are in His sanctuary. . . .
>
> Worship the LORD in holy attire;
> Tremble before Him, all the earth.
> Say among the nations, "The LORD reigns;

Indeed, the world is firmly established, and it will not be moved;
He will judge the peoples with equity."

Let the heavens be glad, and the earth rejoice;
Let the sea roar, and all it contains;
Let the field exult, and all that is in it.
Then all the trees of the forest will sing for joy.

NASB

All about Him!

In his book *Celebration of Discipline,* Richard Foster writes, "The divine priority is worship first, service second. Service flows out of worship. Service as a substitute for worship is idolatry."[9]

We are to worship God before anything else—before worrying about ourselves, before taking Him our lists of problems, before asking for help, before thanking Him for what He has given us, and even before doing things *for* Him!

Worship is all about *Him!* Every instance in Scripture that involves the word *worship* speaks of an action or attitude where thoughts are directed toward God: who He is, what He's done, why He exists, how He thinks, where He is, why He came, and what He wants. It has nothing to do with me. *He* is everything! *He* is . . . whether I'm involved or not.

Okay, now try it. Just adore God alone. Don't mention yourself. Be totally smitten and awed by God—who He is and what He has done—without using any personal pronouns.

Put this book down and try worshiping (focusing on) God. Set a timer or check a clock. Spend the next five minutes focused and fixed only on God, every thought adoring Him. Don't mention yourself once as you talk to Him. Keep your mind, eyes, and heart on Him.

So how did you do?

The first time I tried this exercise, I failed miserably. I remember exactly where I was—sitting in our kitchen, looking through the sliding glass doors into our backyard. Alas, I confess I ran out of things to say before my five-minute timer sounded. In fact, my mind had already wandered to the dirty glass on the doors, the empty flower bed, and an unfinished grocery list.

> Dear God,
>
> You are cool. You are really, really, super, super, super awesome.
>
> Love, Noah B., age 6

Worship takes practice and discipline; it needs to be explained, demonstrated, and taught.

At its very core, worship is our recognition of the greatness of God. All glory should be to Him alone. He requires it from those who know Him.

Psalm 50:7–15 tells the nature of true worship. It states that God is not concerned with rituals and sacrifices; He most desires heartfelt thanksgiving and adoration toward Him. We are to adore Him.

Let's look at some more Scripture passages regarding worship:

Psalm 10:16: "The Lord is King for ever and ever" (KJV).

Psalm 11:7: "The righteous Lord . . ." (KJV).

Psalm 19:7–9: "The law of the Lord is perfect. . . . The statutes of the Lord are right, . . . the commandment of the Lord is pure. . . . The fear of the Lord is clean, . . . the judgments of the Lord are true and righteous altogether" (KJV).

Psalm 24:8: "Who is this King of glory? The Lord strong and mighty, the Lord mighty in battle" (KJV).

Psalm 92:5, 8: "O Lord, how great are thy works! . . . But thou, Lord, art most high for evermore" (KJV).

Psalm 95:1–6: "O come, let us sing unto the Lord . . . for the Lord is a great God, and a great King above all gods. . . . O come, let us worship and bown down: let us kneel before the Lord our maker" (KJV).

Psalm 96:3–4: "Declare his glory among the heathen. . . . For the Lord is great, and greatly to be praised" (KJV).

Psalm 100: "Make a joyful noise unto the Lord, all ye lands. . . . Know ye that the Lord he is God. . . . Enter into his gates with thanksgiving, and into his courts with praise: be thankful unto him, and bless his name. For the Lord is good; his mercy is everlasting; and his truth endureth to all generations" (KJV).

Psalm 105:1: "Give thanks unto the LORD; call upon his name" (KJV).

Exodus 15:1: "I will sing to the LORD, for He is highly exalted" (NASB).

Deuteronomy 32:3–4: "Ascribe greatness to our God! The Rock! His work is perfect, for all His ways are just; a God of faithfulness and without injustice" (NASB).

Daniel 2:20–22: "Blessed be the name of God for ever and ever: for wisdom and might are his: And he changeth the times and the seasons. . . . He revealeth the deep and secret things: he knoweth what is in the darkness, and the light dwelleth with him" (KJV).

Malachi 2:1: "If you do not set your heart to honor my name, . . . I will send a curse upon you."

Did you notice the authors never mention themselves? Over and over Scripture tells us what is meant by the act of worship. We are even told exactly what to say in worship. All focus is on God! Worship is looking at God alone.

In a sermon entitled "Why Worship?" author and pastor Max Lucado says, "Never has one phrase rerouted my life more than a phrase a friend shared with me at a conference: 'It's not about me, and it's not about now.' Scripture tells us from the first page through the last; it's all about God and His Glory."[10] He goes on to explain God's preeminence. "God is higher than anything. He is higher than anything remotely associated with this life or us. When we truly worship, we declare God's glory, and it takes the attention off ourselves, centering it where it should be."[11]

Worship is thinking on purpose, with a genuine heart interest and knowledge about God.

Let's look at knowledge. In Luke 6:40, Jesus said, "Everyone who is fully trained will be like his teacher." Paul said, "Since we live by the Spirit, let us keep in step with the Spirit" (Gal. 5:25). "So Paul stayed for a year and a half, teaching them the word of God" (Acts 18:11).

Once again, nothing is said about age, stage in life, or convenience. Worship is not multiple choice. It's our responsibility. If we belong to God, we have a job and a job description. Our job is to point to Him.

Let's say you're a tour guide for some expansive, lush gardens. (I immediately visualize the glorious Huntington Library botanical gardens in San Marino, California.) Your responsibility is to become educated on the grounds' gardens, diverse vegetation, and history to benefit those who take the tour.

After a few weeks, not only have you mastered details and data, you are quite good at what you do. Your people skills have surprised even you. You're quickly developing the reputation of being the most sought-after tour guide on staff.

Soon you realize it would be much less trouble simply to *tell* people about the gardens instead of walking them around. Much larger crowds could be served by installing a sound system at the front gate. You could entertain and show off your vast expertise without taking a step. You are a genius!

However, your boss hired you to show the remarkable grounds, not to tell people about them. Visitors have come to see the gardens, and you have gotten in the way.

We need to be reminded that we are not here for people to notice how remarkable we are. While on this planet, our job description is to worship and glorify God. We are tour guides, showing the world *His* unspeakable glory. And we need to get out of the way. The act of worship clarifies our role.

I grew up on stage. By the fourth grade, I had starred in my first play. Today is no different! I still love speaking and performing. Nevertheless, I shudder to think how many times I

> Dear God,
>
> You made such a beautiful world. You wrote a GREAT book. You are the one and only true Heavenly Father and I'll see you in a few years. You really like kids a lot—that's cool. It's all about You. It's not about us.
>
> Love, Bryce B., age 8

have been that well-spoken tour guide in the way of others' seeing God's glory.

As a child of God, my only job is to worship Him and help others see His beauty and saving grace. Our job is to reflect His glory so people see *Him!*

Tomorrow start spending five minutes each morning looking at God alone, giving all glory and worship to Him. List as many attributes as you can remember. List His creations. It gets much easier the more you do it. Soon you won't have to set your timer. I promise your life will never be the same again.

Then introduce this concept to a child.

If children spend five minutes a day worshiping and adoring Almighty God, it will become part of who they are and who they grow to be. They will fall in love. It will begin the lifelong process that will forever glue them to God.

3

HERO WORSHIP

The Example

> Then the LORD will scatter you among all nations, from one end of the earth to the other. There you will worship other gods—gods of wood and stone, which neither you nor your fathers have known. Among those nations you will find no repose, no resting place for the sole of your foot. There the LORD will give you an anxious mind, eyes weary with longing, and a despairing heart. You will live in constant suspense, filled with dread both night and day, never sure of your life.
>
> Deuteronomy 28:64–66

The first verse I memorized as a child was John 3:16. Then I learned the Ten Commandments. The "thou shalt nots" were indelibly impressed on my brain.

The first commandment is "Thou shalt have no other gods before me" (Exod. 20:3 KJV). That is followed by "You shall not make for yourself an idol in the form of anything in heaven above or on the earth beneath or in the waters below. You shall not bow down to them or worship them; for I, the LORD your God, am a jealous God, punishing the children for the sin of the fathers to the third and fourth generation . . ." (Exod. 20:4).

Whew, lucky for me, I thought. I would never have to worry about worshiping an idol. Where would I get an idol, anyway? Besides, Mom and Dad would never allow something like that in our house. No bowing down to idols for me!

Then I became smitten with pop singer Pat Boone. While reading a fan magazine at my best friend Jannet's house, I sent away for information on his fan club.

To me, Pat Boone was the most handsome guy on the face of the earth. I loved his voice. My favorite song, of course, was "April Love." And then I received the newsletter, complete with a list of his hobbies, his family information, and an auto-graphed picture of him clad in his trademark white suit and white shoes. Be still my heart!

I read every word of the newsletter a dozen times. I memo-rized every detail. No one made me. I wanted to stare at his picture and learn all I could about this popular, famous, fas-cinating singer. Funny, isn't it? We never met, and he never knew I existed. He never did one thing for me. I adored him nonetheless.

However frivolous this illustration is, it makes for a perfect example of what worship should entail: adora-tion—just because. It also shows that kids are capable of worship. Our task is to direct their worship toward God.

When my lovable nephew Andy was eleven years old, he "introduced" me to his hero—Don Mattingly, left-handed first baseman for the New York Yankees. Although this wasn't a physical meeting, I got to know this player in great detail.

Andy shared his assortment of Mattingly memorabilia, including his prized collection of baseball cards. I

> *Dear God,*
>
> *You make wonderful cats and hamsters. Thank you for making families. Thank you for money that helps moms and dads buy clothes. You make wonderful mountains and the beach too.*
>
> *Love, Avery M., age 7*

learned every conceivable baseball statistic and thumbed through a maze of photos and newspaper articles. I touched his treasured autograph. I heard blow-by-blow descriptions of Mattingly's best games, and through my nephew I relived each of these brilliant plays.

You get the idea. By the end of an hour, I knew more about this man than I knew about my own husband! The delivery by which my nephew had acquainted me with this champion was spellbinding in itself. He adored this hero and never mentioned himself once.

The interesting part of these two hero-worship relationships is that they were both one-sided. All focus was on the one being worshiped. Pat Boone never knew I existed, and my nephew never met his baseball hero. All adoration was given without any mention of anything in return—a perfect example of what God expects from us.

I fell "in love" dozens of times once I discovered boys sometime after the age of twelve. Admittedly, it was no more than heart flutters, butterflies in the stomach, ogling, and dreaming about them. I remember inconspicuously following them around, trying to get pictures, saving any morsel of a note or scrap of something they had touched.

Basically, I was just being an adolescent, obsessed with a particular gorgeous, wonderful boy . . . until another came along a couple of days later. Believe me, I could sit through an entire class at school and never take my eyes off the boy of my dreams!

I talked on the telephone for hours about my boyfriend of the week. My diary read like a silly romance novel. I was in a constant state of wondering what he thought about, what he was like, what made him laugh, his taste in music, his hobbies, his favorite sport, his favorite color, his favorite food. You get the picture. It was all about him.

My girlfriends and I used to refer to our feelings as "worshiping" the very ground where our current heartthrob walked. In those days, I knew as much as I could possibly learn about the object of my devotion, focus, and worship.

We never mentioned ourselves, never had any reason to include ourselves in the topic of conversation. We never asked

Dear Heavenly Father,

You know everything about me so there's no need for an introduction. Everyone says how amazing you are but they don't know the half of it. Humans wouldn't be here if it weren't for You. When You created the universe, You knew what every second of life would be. Before anyone in this time was born You did the most difficult thing when You sacrificed Your Son Jesus. You put Your own Son on the cross to take away people's sin. You show mercy and love. You love so much more than anyone can imagine. Everything good in life, You provide. Thank you so much for everything You do. You are Almighty.

In Jesus' name, amen.

Jason W., age 13

for anything. We just wanted to be near them—adoration for the sake of adoration.

I had no idea this was what God wanted from me.

That first commandment takes on new meaning when you understand the warning connected to it. Be careful what or whom you choose to worship. God created us as worshiping beings. It comes easily—especially for children!

I have a precious seven-year-old girl in my life. Sarah has a doll collection that rivals the best, and she spends hours playing with her dolls. She can talk endlessly about every detail related to them. I spent an entire evening in her bedroom, being thoroughly entertained with stories and descriptions of each doll and her accompanying accessories.

It was amazing how much information could be stored in such a small brain! It was hard to stop her from talking about them, even when it was time to go home. Notably, her conversation hadn't included herself at all.

I asked Sarah's mom to give her the assignment of writing a worship letter to God. Sarah had a tough time when asked to tell what she loved about God without mentioning herself. Her mom said, after attempting several times to question Sarah, "I'm sorry, but if it's not just about Sarah, it's really hard."

What a contrast.

Perhaps we haven't tapped into what is possible for children when it comes to worship. It is easy for children to worship things that fascinate and interest them.

4

GOD WHO?

In the beginning God . . .

Genesis 1:1

My sixth-grade Sunday school teacher stands out in my memory. I loved Mrs. Ida Mae Webster, and she knew God. I remember believing she must have seen Jesus in person at some point in her life. She knew Him so well it was as if she had eaten breakfast with Him before coming to church. She genuinely *glowed* when she read His words from Scripture and told stories about Him. She had my undivided attention.

She was extremely credible as she taught, because she was a personal friend of God. I never told her how much her walk with God had impacted my life before she passed away. I'll tell her in heaven.

It's impossible to worship anyone or anything when we don't know much about the subject. This is especially true about God. Worship isn't possible without knowing God. And that includes more than knowing *about* God.

So who is God? Don't be so quick to smile at that simple question. How much do the kids in your life or ministry know about Him? Is He interesting enough to warrant a child's worship? More to the point, have we presented Him in such a way that kids are fascinated by Him?

As a small child, I knew a lot about Abraham, Moses, Mary, and Joseph. However, knowing a lot about them did not mean I could worship them. Information doesn't equal worship; the adoration element must be included. Even what I had learned about Pat Boone wouldn't have given me enough material for more than a couple of minutes of worship.

My first *true* love was Duane. What an incredibly talented man he is. A general contractor today, he describes himself as having grown up behind a table saw. He can build anything out of wood, learning this craft by watching his dad and grandfather, both carpenters and woodworkers.

My dad was in sales and wore a suit and tie to work every day. He left clean every morning and returned home clean every night. He was fairly handy around our house, mechanically speaking, but he couldn't actually build things.

The first time I saw Duane build a kitchen, complete with solid oak cabinets, I was amazed. I stood in awe of his talent. Actually, everything he did seemed remarkable to me.

When we first began dating, he handcrafted a beautiful wooden box for me. I remember thinking he deserved a Pulitzer or an Oscar or some other award for his remarkable talent. Everything he made compounded my admiration.

Obviously, my growing love for him affected my behavior and priorities. I wanted to learn everything I could about him—everything! I was eager to discover anything, no matter how seemingly small or insignificant.

In the process, I emulated a sort of worshipful admiration. I talked about him for hours to anyone who would listen. I adored him and focused on him without ever thinking of myself. I didn't care that he came home grimy from his work. I adored him so much. I didn't see anything I didn't like.

What about God? How much do we know about Him? He created everything in this phenomenal, incomparable universe.

Yet it was never my first reaction to stand in awe of God—it never even crossed my mind. God created the tree that produced the wood for that box Duane built. And he made Duane too!

Why didn't I see God's genius or wish for an award for Him? Why couldn't I talk about Him for hours and hours on the phone? Did I not love Him enough? It never occurred to me that God deserves all credit—for everything.

Worshiping God isn't possible without first *knowing* God. Adoration isn't possible without knowing God.

Where do we begin? Knowing a lot *about* God is the first step toward the intimate knowledge needed for true worship. We can begin by studying who God is and what He does.

> Dear God,
>
> You are everything. We praise and worship You for what You do. Our life is to praise You and never let go of prayer. No matter how much people pull away, You never let go. Thank You for being God and never letting go. Amen.
>
> Love, Laura G., age 13

God is the first and the last, the beginning and the end.

He is bigger than all.

He is the creator of all and the keeper of His creation.

He is the architect of the universe and the manager of all time.

He always was. He always is. He always will be.

He is unmoved.

He is unchanged.

He is undefeated.

He was bruised and He was smitten down and beaten, but He is the healer.

He was pierced and yet He takes away pain.

He was persecuted and yet He brings freedom.

He was dead and gives life; He is life.

He is risen and brings power.

He reigns and brings peace.

He is light, love, and Lord.

He is goodness, kindness, and gentleness.

He is holy, righteous, mighty, powerful, and pure.

His ways are right; His Word is eternal. His will is unchanging.

He is Redeemer, Savior, guide, and peace.

He is joy and comfort.

He is the wisdom of the wise, the Ancient of Days, the ruler of rulers, the leader of leaders, and sovereign Lord of all that was and is and is to come.

He forgives.

He is faithful.

His love is unconditional and forever.

He is the Savior of all humankind.

This is the tip of the iceberg. He is all this and so much more. He deserves to be worshiped. He deserves to be worshiped by every child in the world.

So how do we get our kids fascinated by God? Maybe we start by translating who God is and what God does into children's language, something easier for them to understand.

One good topic is God's creation. We tell kids God created everything—*everything*. We assume they understand. But "everything" is vague. Specific things fascinate kids.

Did you know, for instance, that God created clouds? Our son Mark realized clouds were God's idea (and creation) during his second-grade science project. His assignment involved making a big cotton-ball-covered poster, illustrating the three main types of clouds. What a fun project. He was quite impressed with this mysterious phenomenon called a cloud. He wrote all the facts in his notebook and then practiced his demonstration for his dad and me.

When he finished, I remarked how clouds were a funny part of God's creation. It stopped him cold. "It doesn't say anything about clouds in the creation story," he said confidently. Mark knew the creation story from Genesis, so he quoted, "God created the heavens and the earth." (Fortunately, I quickly found Psalm 147:8, which says God put the clouds in the sky.)

I then painstakingly explained how God made many things that were not literally mentioned in the Bible. If He had listed everything, the book would have been too big to carry! However, God is the only one—ever—who creates from nothing. God created everything.

From that day on, Mark thought God was very cool for having made a world with an atmosphere designed to make clouds.

Did you know that the planet Jupiter orbits the sun only once every twelve years and Saturn once every twenty-nine years? Their timing remains accurately on schedule. And did you know that if the South Pole were somehow to move a few miles closer to the sun, we'd all be dead?

Are you aware that all the food we eat comes, directly or indirectly, from plants? Even if we eat nothing but meat, we are still getting food from plants. Of all living things, plants alone can make food. It's intriguing! Humans, with all our technological attempts at processing and manufacturing food, have yet to create something from nothing.

Do you realize that astronomers say there are over a billion stars in the universe! (There could actually be more.) Isaiah 40:26 reads, "Lift up your eyes on high and see who has created the stars, the One who leads forth their host by number, He calls them all by name; because of the greatness of His might and the strength of His power not one of them is missing" (NASB). Wow! God knows them all by name. The fantasy phenomenon Star Wars has yet to out-create God.

A teenager came to our church one week because he was curious about

Dear God,

You are the best King. You made beautiful flowers. You are very kind because You sent Jesus to die on the cross. I will praise You every day. I love you.

Love, Tessa Joy O., age 5

the creator of earthquakes (we live in California). Humans have yet to imitate God.

Think how impressed kids are these days with surround sound and hi-tech amplification of sound systems. Do you realize that Moses made two trumpets out of silver that were more powerful than the amplification in arenas all over our country (see Num. 10:1–2)? They were long, straight tubes, flared at the ends.[1] When Moses blew them, all the children of Israel could hear them—at the least 603,550 people (see Num. 2:32). Now that is unbelievable amplification!

We have such a clever and imaginative God. There are millions of things about Him to teach our kids. Start making your list.

Children are so perceptive. They will sense if we know Him. They sense our adoration and awe when we speak of God or His creation. Are we astonished as we learn His attributes? Do our faces light up when we speak of Him? Children study our response to the very mention of His name.

We recently launched an exciting project in our church's second-through-fifth-grade department. We painted one entire wall blue. Then one-by-one we added various names of God in black. The top corner, in bold print, reads "I Am." That is followed by nearly a hundred names of God. The kids brought in His names, with accompanying Scripture references, qualifying each one as it was added to the wall.

Realizing that just having the names on the wall would not accomplish the intended result, we established the "God wall challenge." The challenge took place between services one Sunday morning. We offered a prize of one dollar per name to the child who wrote from memory the most names of God. Our winner was Jonathan, age eight, who wrote fifty-one names, earning a

> Dear God,
>
> You are so great! You made everything. You made the heavens and the earth. You care for people and You give families that are loving. I love You Lord!
>
> Love, Ashlyn O., age 6

whopping fifty-one dollars! Our pastor had him recite the names in church the following week.

Six months later, the children offered the God wall challenge to the entire congregation.

The children's division winner was nine-year-old Rachel, who rattled off eighty-seven names of God from memory. She beat the entire pastoral staff, the elders, and the deacons! Miss Diane, our fifth-grade Sunday school teacher, took the adult division honors with ninety-four names. Some of the names were as follows:

Abba—Romans 8:15
Almighty—Psalm 68:14
Alpha—Revelation 22:13
author of life—Acts 3:15
Beginning and the End—Revelation 21:6
Branch—Jeremiah 33:15
bread of life—John 6:35
bridegroom—Isaiah 62:5b
bright Morning Star—Revelation 22:16
chosen one—Isaiah 42:1
Christ—Matthew 22:42
Comforter—John 14:26 (KJV)
Counselor—John 14:26
Creator—1 Peter 4:19
deliverer—Romans 11:26
door—John 10:7 (KJV)
eternal God—Deuteronomy 33:27
Everlasting Father—Isaiah 9:6
Father—Matthew 6:9
friend—James 2:23; John 3:29
God—Genesis 1:1
good shepherd—John 10:11
guard—2 Timothy 1:12

guide—Psalm 48:14

Holy One—Acts 2:27

Holy Spirit—John 14:26

hope—Titus 2:13

Immanuel—Isaiah 7:14

jealous—Exodus 20:5

Jehovah—Psalm 83:18 (KJV)

Jesus—Matthew 1:21

judge—Acts 10:42

king—Zechariah 9:9

King of kings—1 Timothy 6:15

Lamb of God—John 1:29

life—John 14:6

light of the world—John 8:12

Lion of the tribe of Judah—Revelation 5:5

living water—John 4:10

Lord—John 13:13

Lord of lords—1 Timothy 6:15

love—1 John 4:8

Master—Luke 5:5

Messiah—John 4:25

Omega—Revelation 22:13

peace—Ephesians 2:14

Physician—Luke 4:23

potter—Jeremiah 18:6

power of God—1 Corinthians 1:24

prophet—Acts 3:22

Redeemer—Job 19:25

rock—1 Corinthians 10:4

ruler—Revelation 3:14

Savior—Luke 2:11

servant— Isaiah 42:1

shield—Genesis 15:1

stone—1 Peter 2:8
Teacher—John 13:13
truth—John 14:6
vine—John 15:5
way—John 14:6
wisdom of God—1 Corinthians 1:24
Wonderful Counselor—Isaiah 9:6
Word—John 1:1

This is a great start. Knowing God's names introduces volumes of information about Him. Listing His attributes works too. However, knowing His names and attributes isn't worship. All the knowledge in the world isn't the answer.

Understanding His names and attributes comes next. *Bridegroom* triggered questions the day it graced the wall. How interesting! The kids wanted to know why God (in the form of Jesus) was referred to as a bridegroom. That took almost an hour to explain!

Then kids asked about *bread of life, physician, rock, vine, shepherd, Counselor, jealous, Creator,* and more! That's six months' curricula right there!

Listing God's names and understanding and *believing* them to be true, with genuine gratitude and heartfelt adoration, makes up worship. Wanting to know more about Him, wanting to spend every minute talking about who He is and what He does, is worship.

Let's look at adoration for the sake of adoration.

How do we explain to children the idea of adoring God? Perhaps if they knew how much God desires this adoration, it would penetrate their hearts. Do you know any children who would rather spend time adoring and worshiping God than doing anything else?

A good illustration comes from an inner-city pastor who attended one of my worship seminars. He told how he placed a napkin of salty potato chips on kids' chairs before they arrived for church one morning. Since most of the kids came with empty stomachs, the chips were quickly gobbled up.

Then as he started teaching the morning's lesson, he began pouring water into paper cups in front of the classroom. The kids were so parched from the salty chips that they simply couldn't be quiet and listen to the lesson. They kept interrupting him, asking for a drink. He tried distracting them but to no avail. They were just too thirsty!

Finally, he stopped the lesson and asked, "Are you so thirsty you can't listen or think of anything but a drink of water?"

"Yes!" they answered in unison.

He had made his point. "This is exactly what God wants from us," he told the children. "He is a jealous God, wanting us so thirsty for His living water (Him) that we can think of nothing else!" (See Matt. 5:6.)

> Dear God,
>
> You are the greatest weatherman. People who watch TV don't even know it. You know everything from rain to tornados that are going to happen first. You see everywhere around the world and you do it at one time. You thought it all up in the first place. You are smarter than anyone in the universe.
>
> Love, Sam K., age 10

This is the kind of adoration God wants! What a great worship moment focusing on what God wants! There is so much to learn as we fall in love.

Kids need to discover the million fascinating things written about our awesome God. We want them so taken with Him that they *glow* when they talk about Him! Do we glow when we teach about Him? When is the last time you got goose bumps explaining God to someone? When was the last time just thinking of His greatness and love caused tears to stream down your face?

September 11, 2001, is a date forever etched in our memories. The emotional response that rained across our country was something I have never before experienced. In Southern California, I watched how the tragedy—some three thousand miles away—affected the children of our church. On the first anniversary of the attack, I spoke with one of those children, who cried as she related how bad she still feels for all those kids left parentless. She couldn't understand how "hate" could cause all this pain. I know children are capable of deep feelings when they truly understand the concept or consequence of a truth shown to them. How deeply do our kids feel about God? Have your kids ever shed tears over the things of God?

The older my dad got, the more emotional he was as he prayed or talked about God. I remember thinking at first that it was just his age. Actually, it was his relationship with God that altered the last ten years of his life. Until he retired he was too busy with "the everyday stuff" to get into God's Word on a daily basis. When he began teaching a church class for young married couples, his passion and heart for God noticeably changed. He cried easily over the things of God.

When was the last time you cried because someone used the Lord's name in vain? Has your heart ever been broken as you've humbled yourself before this awesome God?

In 2 Kings 20:5, God says, "I have heard your prayer, I have seen your tears; I will heal you." David says in Psalm 126:5, "Those who sow in tears will reap with songs of joy." In Isaiah 38:5, God tells Hezekiah, "I have heard your prayer and seen your tears; I will add fifteen years to your life." Tears show a depth of emotion obvious to God as well as those around us.

Lamentations is a book of mourning, expressing the anguish of the Jews at the sight of the utter ruin of their city, their temple, and their people. It's written in the form of poetry, an art form bursting with emotion. Lamentations 2:18–19 is a prayer for the children who were starving to death: "Let your tears run down like a river day and night; give yourself no relief; let your eyes have no rest. . . . Pour out your heart like water before the presence of the LORD. Lift up your hands to Him for the life of your little ones who are faint because of hunger" (NASB). There is a gut-wrenching element to crying. It expresses deep and intense passion over something.

Children cry easily over things like not getting their way. Tears may flow during a tantrum, yet how many children cry because their friends don't love God like they do? How many tears are shed in the name of God?

Luke 7:44 describes a woman who washed the feet of Jesus with her tears. You can bet it wasn't just a drop or two. I'll venture a guess—the tears were a result of being overwhelmed by God's presence.

Tears show a deeper level of emotion than even the most eloquently spoken words.

What do our kids cry over? What do our kids care deeply about? What gets their attention? What is important to our kids? What do they know? Let's find out about the children in our lives.

Hold your own focus group. Write some questions. Pass them out to all your church kids. Explain that answers aren't right or wrong and questionnaires may be filled out anonymously.

Ask about God—who He is, what He has done, what He says, why He has made things a certain way, what makes Him happy or sad, and what His favorite musical instrument might be (Scripture mentions "strings" a lot). Ask what they suppose His favorite color is and why. What is His favorite animal? See how much they can write on their own—just about God.

Be prepared for some discouragement in the beginning. Most kids know very little about God. Create a very simple questionnaire—something like this to start:

1. Who is God?
2. What are several things you love most about Him?
3. What does He specialize in? (What is He known for?)

These are great questions for kids age four and up!

You'll find that if these same questions are asked about the latest craze, cartoon character, music, or sports team, young people are able to provide a wealth of information. Kids know a great deal about things that truly interest and fascinate them!

Remember my nephew Andy and his baseball player? He really *knew* this athlete, having spent hours and hours focusing on this man's schedule, attributes, record-breaking stats, and best plays. Remember Sarah? By age seven she was a marketing agent for her particular dolls!

Yes—this knowledge coupled with focused adoration is worship!

Oh, that our children would know that much about Almighty God! Oh, that they would know Him so well they could talk for hours about Him!

Is this possible? Absolutely! However, it has to be taught.

Teach children how to *know* God. Introduce them to electrifying Bible stories and help them understand His astounding attributes. Focus on His unbeatable "stats" and amazing feats. Encourage them to read books and visualize and sense the intensity with which God loves each of us. Kids need to learn His emotions—what makes God happy or what breaks His heart. There should be excitement and awe at the chance to talk to Him.

To set the foundation, children need to fall in love with Jesus at an early age. They need to be in an atmosphere where it's second nature to seek Him first in life situations.

When I was ten, my mom got a wood-burning set as a Christmas gift. She proceeded to etch Bible verses in wood valances that decorated our kitchen windows. "Jesus is the Bread of Life" adorned our breakfast area.

Soon after, she bought the Bible on records! We listened to a man's smooth voice read Scripture for years until the records suspiciously disappeared. (I'm convinced my brother hid them.) But Mom had the right idea. She had God's words hanging all over our house and echoing off the walls. I'm certain there were days when big band tunes would have been her preference, but she was determined that we would know God.

Moses seems to have more to say about God's instructions regarding our children than almost anyone else in Scripture. Consider again what Moses wrote in Deuteronomy 6:4–9 as I give my own modern translation to these verses: "Bombard your kids with stories and teachings about God and His Word! Do it any way you can, but make it exciting, powerful, and constant! Talk about God first thing in the morning. Write

His names on the kitchen (or church school) wall or ceiling! Talk about God on the way to school. Play Christian music in the car. Put notes in their lunch boxes, reminding them of God's love. Pray over homework. Pray before every meal. Pray to this wonderful God before they go to bed at night. Make Him as much a part of their existence as eating and sleeping. Make them so in awe of God they want to nominate Him for a Pulitzer! Teach them to list His statistics! Help your children to *know* and *adore* God" (author's paraphrase).

Oh, that every child could say, "I know the One I have believed in. I am sure he is able to take care of what I have given him. I can trust him with it until the day he returns as judge" (2 Tim. 1:12 NIrV).

We have a generation of "God who?" kids growing up in our churches!

Let's begin answering their question!

PART 2

HOW

5

LEARN THE LANGUAGE!

God looked down from heaven upon the children of men, to see if there were any that did understand, that did seek God.

Psalm 53:2 KJV

Six-year-old Kimberly sang the hymn "He Lives" at full voice. When she got to the chorus, she belted out, "He walks with me and talks with me along Estero Way." That's how she heard it. (The actual words are "He walks with me and talks with me along life's narrow way.") Since Kimberly lived on Estero Road, her parents enjoyed her translation and never corrected her.

We all smile at the cute stories of kids misinterpreting hymn phrases, but what do our kids actually hear in the church classrooms each week? And if they hear it, do they understand it?

One summer, Tommy, age nine, attended a week-long Vacation Bible School. Each day the teacher invited the children to receive Jesus as their Savior, and each day Tommy left without understanding the concept. He had never before heard the terms *saved* or *become a Christian*. On the last day, as Tommy was leaving with his armful of completed crafts, one of the helpers asked him if he had any questions about the week's lessons.

Tommy admitted, "I really didn't understand a lot that was taught this week." So in his own "language," the helper explained how Jesus had come to earth so Tommy could be forgiven of all the bad things he'd ever done. Tommy could go to heaven someday if he would believe that God's Son, Jesus, paid for his sin and if he would accept the gospel story he heard that week. Tommy eagerly gave his life to Jesus once the concept was clarified.

How important is teaching children in their own language? Tommy lived down the street from my grandmother. The week following his profession of faith he drowned in a swimming pool accident. We haven't the luxury of crossing our fingers and hoping kids understand the lessons week after week. The significance of their relationship with God is critical.

Communicating Vital Concepts

Salvation and worship are the two most important areas that need "translating" in our teaching today.

1. Salvation

A child's need for a personal relationship with Jesus is foremost. As teachers, we are limited in the amount of time we have to tell the gospel story, so in the allotted time, *salvation* should be our first focus. We expect kids (especially unchurched kids) to assimilate the most important, life-altering information in one or two hours a week. Yet it's possible that half the time they don't hear what is said, or they don't understand what they hear!

The younger the child, the more elementary and basic the language must be. For example, a four-year-old child understands how much his parents love him. God's love becomes a concept he can grasp when he understands that the God who created him loves him even more than his parents do. The next step is to teach him how much God wants to be loved back and how we are to obey everything God wrote in His letter to us (the Bible). Since children naturally love their parents, the concept of loving God is logical. Open a Bible and let children look at the truth of God's words, whether they can read or not. Show younger children where the lesson is written. Most are visual and/or tangible learners, and showing them will solidify your point.

> Dear God,
>
> How do you make apples? You probably know everyone likes them. Thank you for making dogs too.
>
> Love, Monica D., age 4

I've discovered that the words *love, believe, promise,* and *obey* are easily understood by all children, but the phrase "accepting Jesus in your heart" is a difficult concept for younger children. So let's be sensitive to use appropriate language with our kids when explaining salvation.

2. Worship

Next in line of importance is teaching children to know God intimately so they can enthusiastically worship Him and pay homage to Him.

Six-year-old Mackenzie smiled when I asked for a definition of *worship.* "I know—it's what happens in big church."

"Who does it?" I asked. She thought for a few seconds and then answered, "I think the music leader."

Of all the children questioned in the surveys I mentioned before, not one answered that worship is a direct order from God. I also never had to interrupt a child in his or her excitement or enthusiasm when describing worshiping God.

I recently asked seven-year-old Sarah for help as I prepared to teach her class about a worship relationship with God. "Can you picture something glued so tightly to something else that it never gets loose or wants to get loose?" I asked.

"Yes, like the bottom of my new shoes," she said confidently. (The soles of her new black shoes were shiny silver. This was a tangible example fresh in her mind.)

"Perfect," I said. "You wouldn't want to go anywhere without the shoe and its sole stuck together! That's how we are to stick to God, not going *anywhere* without Him!"

I had her explain the concept back to me, and it was even more profound. She smiled and said, "*And* we couldn't go too far if they came apart either, could we!"

By speaking to Sarah in her own language, she thoroughly comprehended the importance of intimacy with God. Staying close to God and thinking about Him all the time creates a worship relationship.

So where do we begin? There are some exercises and concepts that, translated simply, will cause young children to develop this intimacy.

Teach the Names of God

One such exercise is teaching the names of God. Obviously, the younger the child, the simpler the names you introduce. *Love* is one of the first names a preschool-age child can easily understand. There are many resources for measuring how much learning is possible for a child according to his or her age group. One such resource is *Learning Life Christian Education and the Practice of Faith*.[1] Each church denomination has such material available. (Check with your own church resources.)

Alpha and Omega means the beginning and the end. Sound too difficult for a first grader to understand? Spend a few minutes with six-year-olds chatting about how God was here before anything or anyone else. Watch the children's eyes get bigger and bigger as they ask, "Was He here before the streets and the houses?" "Was God here before the stars and even Grandpa and Grandma?"

Our son John was what we referred to as "the wonderer" as he grew up. He wondered at length about most things. When this Alpha-Omega conversation came up, his questions continued for days. Out of the blue he would ask, "But was God here before there was air to breathe?" Then, "How did He live without breathing?" We noticed that the more he asked questions, with every answer we gave him, the more in awe of God he became.

Teach the Attributes of God

Another important area to translate is God's attributes. We must make it clear how these characteristics are truly significant in their daily lives. The word *advocate* is a great example (1 John 2:1 KJV). Jesus Christ is our advocate. He is completely devoted to us. He is our supporter, our backer, and our defender. An eight-year-old can understand what *advocate* means! Courtroom stories are so prevalent on TV today that most children know more about prosecuting and defense attorneys than I do! How cool is this? Jesus is our defense attorney, and there is no one who can beat Him!

Always follow up with questions, questions, and more questions! Just like I did with Sarah, ask children to repeat what they heard you say: "Do you think God defends us because we are His children?" "Does God defend us because He loves us?"

Ask Questions

Questions are vital to ensuring that children grasp the definition of *worship*.

1. Ask who God is and what *worship* means to them.
2. Ask them to tell you about the last time they worshiped God.
3. Ask them about God's names and attributes.
4. Ask if they understand clearly how they can come into God's presence at any time. Do they realize they can comfortably talk to Him in their own words?

The more they learn and understand about Almighty God, the more you'll begin to notice an excited anticipation. Yes, *kids* are able to worship God! Yes, *a child* can focus on God alone and get it!

Understanding Learning Styles

Do we know what our children are spiritually grasping on a weekly, monthly, or yearly basis? Can we teach so the message will stick in their hearts? Will they get it when we teach the meaning of worship from God's Word?

Children have diverse learning styles that affect how or what they hear. There are many opinions on how many learning styles actually exist, but the four basic ones that I've found valuable in teaching theater are visual, kinetic, language, and logical.

1. *Visual learners* need to see things. They like to see colors and objects, and they learn through images. For example, they love to watch Bible stories being acted out.
2. *Kinetic learners* process knowledge through physical sensations. They communicate with body language and gestures. They like to participate in musical choreography and actually *do*, rather than watch, the acting in dramas.
3. *Language-oriented learners* think in words and verbalize concepts. They are great tellers of Bible stories.

Dear God,

Worship means just talking about you. I don't know a lot yet, but I know that you are God. You made everything and did it just like that. You sent Jesus to die on the cross for everyone, even the crooks and jerks on the Earth.

You are hard to imagine because you are invisible. The way people know about you is if they go to church, read the Bible or just look at the world.

Yours truly, John T., age 11

4. *Logical learners* think conceptually. They are the "wonderers" who ask all the questions.

Spiritual giftedness, personalities, and various temperaments also have an impact on how kids learn and respond to learning. If you teach the same lesson to ten kids at the same time, each will digest the material differently!

Six-year-olds will not get the same meaning from a lesson as nine-year-olds. Consider the following: Two sisters had the same teacher for children's church. The lesson was about the feeding of the five thousand from Luke 9. The six-year-old told her folks their lesson was about a little boy who shared his lunch and how we should learn that Jesus wants us to share. Her nine-year-old sister said their lesson was about Jesus performing miracles. They had the same teacher and the same lesson, but they arrived at a different understanding.

Have you ever heard of a sermon that *every* adult in the congregation processed exactly the same way? A senior pastor has staggering odds against him. During a year's worth of sermons, parishioners hear only half the intended messages (and personally apply even fewer of those), though they faithfully sit through every service.

Look at a few of the variables involved in an audience of one hundred adults: age, economic and educational differences, spiritual maturity, gender, stress levels, fatigue, and health. Different people hear the same sermon in very different ways. The best way to know if a person understands a message is to ask follow-up questions. The pastor is at a disadvantage because he lacks question-and-answer time.

The same variables are true for an audience of children, but we can ask questions. Where children are involved, so much is at stake! If we don't reach kids for Jesus by the age of twelve, the likelihood of ever doing so is slim.

When I think of all the "lessons" our kids hear in age-appropriate church classes without having a clue what they mean, I shudder. Imagine what they don't grasp sitting in an adult church service! We assume far too much when it comes to children's interpretation of spiritual and biblical language.

Dear God,

You are so awesome. You made this wonderful world and all the wonderful people and animals. You are always here and not just on Sunday. Hopefully this makes You very happy. Hopefully You like all the singing and hand clapping people do in church to worship You. Mr. Sheehan is a great praise and worship leader who teaches great songs to sing about You. Hopefully You're not sad that all people don't feel like this, but maybe someday they will.

You are very special to me. I love you.

Justin W., age 10

Recently, a seven-year-old girl announced to her parents that she wasn't going to pray anymore! Surprised, since prayer had been a big part of their everyday family life, her parents asked why she would say such a thing. She explained, "Why should I talk to God when He never talks to me?"

She assumed God spoke aloud to her mom and dad. All other adults in her life referred to things God had told them, but she had never once heard Him talk. She had tried her best to hear God speak but had failed to hear His voice. So she decided to quit talking to Him.

Many children get lost in adult vocabulary. Their maturing in the Lord stops the moment they accept Jesus.

We waste so many valuable years because kids don't comprehend what we say in church. My Christian experience was only somewhat important to me as a child. I liked going to my classes at church, and unlike some of my friends, I never rebelled against attending. It was a nice, social, predictable part of my existence.

When I was six years old, I accepted Jesus, asking Him to "come into my heart." I really understood it because my parents painstakingly explained it to me. (However, one of my friends was frightened at the thought of someone cutting her chest open to get into her heart!)

I remember having the act of baptism carefully explained to me as well. The same ritual ensued when I wanted to take part in communion. Those three areas had clarity.

The majority of the other "Christianese" spoken by my parents and church leaders lost a lot in the translation on the way from my ears to my brain.

We are, as teachers and parents, interpreters of God's Word, translating it into a child's language. We are dictionaries defining things and encyclopedias explaining things to help children know God better—enabling them to worship Him.

We may have to repeat and vary the process many times. Every child is different. Each one grasps information at his or her level of understanding. Therefore, in talking about spiritual truths, we need to turn around immediately and *ask* each child what was just said.

God's Word in Kids' Language

I believe God's Word is holy, inspired, and infallible, and it will never return void. It's probably even more powerful in its original Greek and Hebrew—but we want our kids to get it *today!* We want to touch their innermost hearts, helping them understand God's truths as *they* read His Word. Two of my favorite translations that speak the language of a five-, eight-, or twelve-year-old are The New International Reader's Version and the International Children's Bible.

Example: Genesis 1:1–2

The New King James (adult) reads, "In the beginning God created the heavens and the earth. The earth was without form, and void; and darkness was on the face of the deep. And the Spirit of God was hovering over the face of the waters."

The International Children's Bible reads, "In the beginning God created the sky and the earth. The earth was empty and had no form. Darkness covered the ocean, and God's Spirit was moving over the water."

Example: 1 John 1:9

The King James Version (adult) reads, "If we confess our sins, he is faithful and just to forgive us our sins, and to cleanse us from all unrighteousness."

The New International Reader's Version (children's) reads, "But God is faithful and fair. If we admit that we have sinned, he will forgive us our sins. He will forgive every wrong thing we have done. He will make us pure."

It's much easier for children to stay interested when they can easily decipher the passage of Scripture.

One Sunday morning after his teacher read a passage from Psalms to the class, six-year-old Bryce asked, "Why didn't God write a Bible for kids too?"

Twenty years ago, my then eight-year-old son Mark begged, "Please, don't read the boring parts we don't understand."

When I was a child, the Bible's big, complicated words never seemed to apply to me either. Scripture always sounded so very grown-up, so proper, so adult, and so religious. The words *thee* and *thou* made no sense to me. I was positive the Bible was not for kids.

Knowing God's Word and worshiping God spiritually transforms lives. We can help kids experience unparalleled richness in their walk with God—that is, if they can understand what it means! Let's not assume anything when it comes to a kid's grasp of spiritual things.

Are we speaking a foreign language when we teach our kids in church? Let's learn the language kids understand and teach God's Word so they get it!

6

THE ART OF FOCUS

Pay attention to what I say; listen closely to my words. Do not let them out of your sight, keep them within your heart.

Proverbs 4:20–21

Worship demands focus. Focus requires a self-initiating drive, an act of the will, a "want to," not just compliant cooperation.

Performing in theater requires many forms of discipline for kids, but the most important is *focus*. *Webster's Dictionary of Everyday Use* defines *focus* as "a bonding of sorts; a desire to look closely at something; concentrating on purpose; studying; converging."

Focusing during every second of the play is essential. From the minute the curtain rises until the final line has been delivered, focus is required.

One of my favorite stories about focus on stage involves our daughter, Nancy, who was eleven years old at the time. Her role in a Christmas play required that she "sleep" on a bed, center stage, during the first scene. On the night of the performance, the stage lights were very warm, and so were her cozy flannel pajamas. At the close of the first scene, she didn't respond to her next cue. She had actually fallen asleep in the bed! The backstage manager had to walk center stage and wake her up—much to the delight of the audience. The following three performances that weekend, Nancy remained extremely focused—not to mention awake—the entire time, and the play went off without a hitch.

Jay, a determined eight-year-old, arrived at a matinee performance with a tummyache. His mom wasn't sure if it was nerves or a legitimate illness, but Jay, who had a lead role, wanted to go on. The stomach trouble hit—without much warning—two minutes before he was to sing his solo. He ran off the stage, threw up outside, ran back, and sang his solo.

That day gave new meaning to the phrase "The show must go on." Not only was he focused, but the determination and the "want to" were obvious! Worshiping God requires purposeful focus coupled with "want to."

Leonard Sweet's book *Soul Salsa* discusses our multitask way of life, or as he calls it, "'stacking'—doing two or three things at once, purposely focused on each, as we live life these days."[1]

"Stacking" is a way of life for my grown children. I'm amazed to see how they can work on a computer, talk on the phone, eat dinner, and do whatever else while watching television simultaneously!

Sweet goes on to say, "If truth be told, 'full attention' moments are few and far between—when they do occur, it's called 'worship.'"[2]

Exactly! Worship is an act of the will, giving "full attention moments" to God. Worship is concentrating on God on purpose because we want to.

Dear God,

You are such a big God. You are like nothing else because You are so big and awesome. You gave us this big world to play baseball in. Do You like the songs we sing to You in church? Hopefully they make You smile.

You and Jesus are my special friends. I love you.

Sidney W., age 8

It's choosing to turn our eyes on Him and look closely—to study Him, hear what He says, and focus completely.

The topic of children's ability to focus may conjure up all sorts of uneasy feelings, especially those with preschool children, to be sure.

Although adorable and extremely bright, my eight-year-old Mark seemed to be focus challenged. Soccer was a disaster. One minute he'd be focused on the game and the next minute crouched in the grass examining a bug or a piece of trash.

His teacher informed us that this occurred daily at school, generating even greater concern. We sought professional counsel to see if there was a serious problem. The doctor sent us home with an assignment. We were to time how long Mark could sit in front of a TV program.

The next morning this same easily distracted boy sat mesmerized in front of *Mr. Rogers' Neighborhood* for a full thirty minutes. Even the most preoccupied child has the potential for a few consecutive moments of focus. Admittedly, most young children require entertainment to keep their interest, but sadly, so do most adults.

My husband enjoys football and finds it entertaining enough to watch for hours. I have trouble focusing on football games for more than five minutes. Nevertheless, out of my self-sacrificing love for him, I make an attempt. Focusing on a football game, no matter how often I try, will never be second nature to me. The initial bond is not there—no particular love connection, no potential reward, and no "want to." In other words, when it comes to giving attention to football, I make myself do it.

Guess what? Self-initiated focusing, without enticements, is almost a lost art. Most of the time we must be entertained or bribed in order to focus. However, God tells us we are to worship Him—not multiple choice, not negotiable! Our response is obedience.

To obey God, we must worship Him. Worship requires focus. In the beginning, worshiping God may require a deliberate act of obedience. As knowledge grows and passion for God deepens, the ability and desire to worship come more easily.

When people fall in love, no one needs to command them to focus on the object of their love! It's automatic. In fact, it's usually all they can think about.

Sound simple? No, sorry, this part is not. Unless we *work* at keeping our relationship with God alive and growing, it won't happen. I don't rely on the heart flutters I experienced when I met Duane over thirty years ago to keep our relationship strong. Marriage is a work in progress at all times. Unless we worship God more and more routinely, discovering new truths daily, it's easy to fall back into old patterns of neglect. We'll unconsciously wonder what *we* will get out of it.

A difficult obstacle in teaching worship to children is their natural tendency to be self-centered and overindulged. Children are born this way. Then every parent and grandparent involved in a child's life perpetuates that self-centeredness.

Think about it. Every time you talk to a child, how does your conversation begin? "How are you?" "What did you do at school today?" "Where did you get those beautiful eyes?" "Where did you get those new shoes?" In fact, we all respond easily to questions about ourselves.

But worship is about God!

This is why children must be taught, step-by-step, to care about God. After they understand His amazing uniqueness, we teach them—over and over and over again—to dwell on these qualities every day, to take their eyes off themselves and put them on God for five minutes a day.

This is a brand-new concept for kids. It's not about them. It's not even about how they feel or how much they love God. Worship is not what the child does for God. Worship is only about God. Children are to give all focus to God alone, the same as adults. So how can we teach a child to focus?

Directing a Child's Focus

Deliberate questions are one way to direct a child's focus. "What kind of sky did God make this morning?" "Which of God's birds did you see today?" "I wonder why God made smiles." "Did you know God picked the tune birds sing?" "Do you wonder how many of God's animals can sing?" "I wonder what God is thinking about right now." Directing children to focus on God alone leads them toward worship.

Silence is another powerful tool for creating focus. It works miracles on stage. We want deliberate silence, not the uncomfortable silence of someone forgetting a line. An actor can freeze time, holding an audience spellbound by using intentional silence on stage. And it works in developing focus for worship too.

I once watched a rock star being interviewed on a late-night talk show. He said when he steps in front of a large, noisy audience, he doesn't move or make a sound for forty seconds. The screams are deafening during the first twenty or thirty seconds. If he remains perfectly still and silent for forty seconds, the audience quiets and just stares at him, and you can hear a pin drop amid a crowd of thousands. He has them in his control as they wait to see what he will do or say. At this point he can speak in a whisper and everyone will hear him. The silence forces the audience to focus on him. He knows the power of focus.

Worship is often associated with quiet. Silence is an especially helpful tool in teaching children to focus. I'm certain most people realize that children learn about focus differently than adults. The reason is simple: As I mentioned before, from the time children are born, everything revolves around them and their immediate wants and needs.

Worship is about God. Acts 15:12 says, "Then all the multitude kept silent and listened to Barnabas and Paul declaring how many miracles and wonders God had worked through them among the Gentiles" (NKJV). A moment of silence before looking at God is a powerful teaching moment. (See chapter 10 for more on the concept of silence used in worship.)

Dear God,

You hear every need and You have a purpose for everything. You created all the earth. You love everyone, even those who are on the wrong path.

Love, Ryan F., age 12

I was thrilled to get an e-mail from a woman who attended my Teaching Kids to Worship class in Washington. She wrote,

> Three years ago I attended your class, Teaching Kids to Worship. I had never thought of teaching kids to worship, just leading them in worship. It was soon after your class that a new volunteer in our children's ministry said to me, we really need to TEACH these kids how to worship. I wish you could have seen my face! I got all excited and told her about your workshop. The following week we stopped everything for a moment of silence, focused all the children's attention toward God, and had our first worship moment. It's been three weeks and the kids are so serious about the worship time. I am always amazed at the way the Lord works.

Physically changing positions helps redirect children's attention to enable them to focus on God for worship time. I heard a motivational speaker explain how an element of surprise is the key to altering someone's state (focus). He suggested a sudden body movement, standing or walking away, or an abrupt voice change as methods to interrupt a mental pattern and refocus a person's attention.

In theater we use an unexpected position change, a light change, or a scene change to redirect the audience's focus. It is critical to the flow of the plot for the audience to stay focused as the story progresses. Likewise, a spiritual focus is critical for the future of our children.

Experiment to find the perfect focus tool for your kids. Incorporate some focus exercises in your playtime. Following are three exercises we have used:

1. The freeze exercise. Have all the kids hold a position mid-movement when the teacher says freeze. Reward the child who does it best, first, or longest.
2. The find an object exercise. Have all the kids focused to search for one particular object hidden in the room within a certain time frame.

3. The Where's Waldo exercise. Have the kids look at a picture, studying it to find the inconspicuous hidden within the obvious.

A woman in one of my workshops shared a contest she used in her church. Before the class of four- and five-year-olds began their serious lesson time, they had trouble settling down. So the teachers put a stopwatch on the floor one minute before the story was to begin. The kids who were perfectly quiet by the time the watch sounded got a treat after the lesson. The kids who could repeat the entire lesson at the end of class time got two treats. The collective ability of her class to concentrate, or focus, during lesson time amazed the biggest skeptics! This same focus technique could be used for teaching kids to worship.

I love it. Rewards work for me! Of our three kids, rewards worked best on our youngest, John. Possessing a serious, melancholy temperament, not only did he remember every reward offered, but he tabulated how many I owed him and his siblings for every situation. Whatever works for your kids, use it! Consider the following:

Children learn focus in school.
Homework requires focus.
Music lessons require disciplined focus.
Playing sports requires focus.
Musical theater takes focus.

Why should we settle for less discipline and concentration when it affects kids' relationships with God? Worship is focus on God. It takes discipline, concentration, "want to," and obedience. If we are to obey God's Word, we must teach this truth to our children.

The secrets of their hearts will be brought out into the open. They will fall down and worship God.

1 Corinthians 14:25 NIrV

7

FAMILIARITY

Gather me the people together, and I will make them hear my
words, that they may learn to fear me all the days that they shall
live upon the earth, and that they may teach their children.

Deuteronomy 4:10 KJV

Remember my nephew Andy? Did you wonder how a child
that age could retain so much information about a Yankee first
baseman? In an age when it's difficult to get kids to read books,
how is it possible to glamorize statistics to the point where a
boy would memorize them?

It's mass marketing—brainwashing, familiarizing, repeating
over and over again.

Yes, familiarity actually creates heroes via television, bill-
boards, the Internet, movies, newspapers, music, and magazines. Large amounts of information delivered shrewdly and
skillfully over and over again results in acute familiarity.

If you held up a pair of basketball shoes, I bet most kids in
the room could tell you which player wears that brand and
the slogan of the shoe manufacturer. Companies pay billions

of dollars for child-friendly ads. They know that if you hook children, you have them for life.

James P. Steyer in his spine-chilling *The Other Parent* tells us, "The Teletubbies retailing push, aimed at least indirectly at kids who are crawling and toddling, has really lowered the bar on children's marketing, but some plainly see it as a profitable opportunity. 'The one-to-two-year-old niche hasn't been filled very well,' pointed out Character World's Carol Lowenstine. '*Teletubbies,*' she added enthusiastically, 'is the first brand to come along for this age group on a very large scale, with not only the programming, but all the spin-off products and other marketing elements that will come out of that license.'"[1]

The media brainwashes children into believing they have to have a new favorite toy or hobby. This starts with children as young as one year old! Kids see the product repeatedly—every day, maybe several times a day—on some advertisement, and they know it is their new favorite toy. Brainwashing works!

Several of my elementary-age church kids were recently agog about a new movie. They were so excited that they were finishing each other's sentences. I knew several of their parents, so I asked how many times their children had seen this movie. Zero times! They had seen all the advertisements and hype and were convinced this was their all-time favorite movie.

Steyer also states, "Nancy Shalek, the president of a Los Angeles ad agency, explained, 'Advertising at its best is making people feel that without their product, you're a loser. Kids are very sensitive to that,' she observes. 'If you tell them they'll be a dork if they don't buy something, you've got their attention. You open up emotional vulnerability, and it's very easy to do with kids because they're the most emotionally vulnerable.'"[2]

The world is targeting our children from every possible angle—and doing it on purpose! They are extremely successful, and we can learn from their successes. Teaching must be done *on purpose* over and over and over again.

As parents, we spend hours teaching our children various behaviors. We teach them to eat, walk, talk, read, count, tie their shoes, and dress themselves. We teach them manners, eye

Dear God,

There are many things to thank you for that don't include me. You died on the cross for everyone's sins. You let people into heaven if they just believe that Jesus is your Son and He takes away all sins. You made everything in the whole world and still make new things every day. You love us more than our parents do. You stay awake all the time so you won't miss anything. You are wonderful.

Love always, Carolyn M., age 13

contact, body language, and anything else we deem important. We do it until the habit penetrates the heart and it becomes part of who they are. We want them to grow up and live productively in the culture and customs of our world. Yes, we teach these things over and over again until they have grasped the concept or mastered the ability and it becomes second nature. Children are so easily influenced by what they are exposed to consistently.

Between birth and five years of age, children are more impressionable than at any other time in their lives. They are significantly affected *for life* by what occurs during these first five, formative years.

The next most valuable time slot is between the ages of five and twelve. I won't depress you with the statistics on how hard it is to reach a child after twelve years of age.

We have such a brief period of opportunity to impress children with God's character. We can't overlook this rich opportunity. If it takes familiarity, then let's saturate, immerse, soak, inundate, and engulf our kids with God! Do it over and over again until the habit penetrates the heart and it becomes part of who they are.

Do you know God's idea of familiarity? The prophet Ezekiel was exiled to Babylon by Nebuchadnezzar—along with more than three thousand Jews—and then handed an assignment. God told him to go to the Israelites and shape them up. God was so determined for Ezekiel to know exactly what to say that He handed him a written scroll and instructed him to eat it! God wanted it to become part of him—to be digested (Ezek. 3:1). I suppose that might be considered a somewhat extreme approach today, but God's message was the same then as it is now: "You will know that I am the LORD" (Ezek. 6:7). Children who attend church regularly, who are exposed to a God-centered atmosphere, will be more interested in developing a relationship with Him. The more they love the church experience, the easier it is to penetrate their hearts. However, the church experience alone does not mean they will *naturally* know how to truly worship God.

Worshiping God is the most important element after trusting God as their personal Savior. We help children learn to worship by making God more familiar to them than their sports heroes. This takes practice. It takes consistency.

One avenue to familiarize children with any given subject is music. Billions of dollars are spent yearly in the children's music industry. As evidenced by TV programming from *Sesame Street* to MTV, the world knows how effectively music attracts and holds kids' attention. "At MTV we don't shoot for the 14-year-olds, we own them," said MTV's chairman, Bob Pittman. [3]

Music teaches, stimulates, comforts, persuades, and glues its targeted audience to the desired focal point. If music is this powerful, then let's jump on board!

Music might be the one element that will turn a child's focus toward God and build his or her familiarity with the things of God. A familiar worship song will stay in the heart and on the lips long after the class has

Dear God,

How many fish are in the ocean? You know, don't you. You know everything because you are God. You help all the animals. You love everyone. You are my favorite.

Love, Susan G., age 7

ended. Think of the melodies and lyrics from your childhood that remain with you today. We must utilize every conduit that enables children to know and worship God.

I am saying "we" because I'm preaching to myself as well! For many years, I was primarily concerned with the "production" end of children's ministry—ensuring that weekly programs functioned efficiently. We all know an organized, structured environment is conducive to learning. But I now focus on making an impact rather than being efficient.

Spiritual familiarity doesn't just happen! If a child accepts Jesus as personal Savior at five years of age, wouldn't it be wonderful if he or she automatically acquired a passion and desire to be in God's house? Wouldn't it be thrilling to see a child beg to worship God? It would let us off the hook! Since that doesn't happen, we must teach them what to do next—and then repeat it over and over again.

The act of worship—becoming familiar with God by focusing on Him and His words over and over again—will keep a child loving and walking with God.

Read what one of the greatest authorities on worship, King David, had to say in Psalm 119:

> I rejoice in following your statutes
>   as one rejoices in great riches.
> I meditate on your precepts
>   and consider your ways.
> I delight in your decrees;
>   I will not neglect your word.
>
> verses 14–16

> Your statutes are my delight;
>   they are my counselors.
>
> verse 24

> Let me understand the teaching of your precepts;
>   then I will meditate [focus] on your wonders.
>
> verse 27

For I delight in your commands
　　because I love them.
I lift up my hands to your commands, which I love,
　　and I meditate [focus] on your decrees.

verses 47–48

Your word is a lamp to my feet
　　and a light for my path.

verse 105

Your righteousness is everlasting
　　and your law is true.

verse 142

Let me live that I may praise you,
　　and may your laws sustain me.
I have strayed like a lost sheep.
　　Seek your servant,
　　　　for I have not forgotten your commands.

verses 175–76

The question is no longer, How can we teach children the power of a worship relationship with God? but rather, How can we not? We must give children an opportunity to be so familiar with this knowledge that they will experience a lifelong bond with our Savior.

8

A PLAN FOR WORSHIP

I have set you an example that you should do as I have done for you.

John 13:15

David, age seven, and his family decided to visit a new church. After his Sunday school class was over, David walked with his mother to the car and quietly said, "I don't want to go back there again because the teacher doesn't know what she's doing." When his mother probed further, her son explained, "During our whole class time she kept saying, 'Gee, what should we do next?'"

David was sure his teacher had not prepared for the morning's church lesson. In his mind that translated to, "If the teacher doesn't think the lesson is important, why should I?" As teachers, everything we do and say leaves a lasting imprint, and our effectiveness requires a deliberate plan.

My daughter-in-law Anne teaches fourth grade. The endless hours she spends in lesson planning have resulted in excellent scholastic returns for her students. Anne is well aware that those prestructured schedules are the basis for her success as a teacher. Planning is the key to teaching children to worship as well. There is no such thing as winging it when it comes to the slim window of opportunity we have to teach children.

If we are to glue our children to God, the preparation of a worship program must be on purpose. Some basic guidelines are as follows:

1. Locality is crucial to the process.
2. Teaching must be age appropriate and time sensitive.
3. The instructors need to understand the process.

Set the Stage

Create a worship gathering place, an intriguing location where a child would love to spend time. Find an obviously special element. Make the worship space inviting. Adults can usually worship God in any surrounding. However, a sense of quiet structure helps young children focus more easily and develop a reverence for worshipful moments with God.

When our youngest son, John, was studying for his elementary education teaching credential, he brought home the most interesting books full of the latest teaching techniques. I love reading current manuals just to be sure I'm not missing anything in this area. I was relieved to find that there are still basic rules involved in teaching children a concept or lesson. The "new" teaching systems are not necessarily involved or difficult, but they require *on purpose* planning. Each educational accomplishment requires a plan, a consistent approach, and a schedule. The setting becomes less important as children grow older, but the momentary reverence must always be emphasized.

Set the Time

An hour-long worship service is impossible for children! I've yet to see a young child who could focus on anything for an

Hi God,

Thank you. You are so amazing. Because of you, life works out. You love, lead, teach, comfort and bring justice. You will never abandon your people. You sent Your only Son as the ultimate sacrifice, because people could not, nor ever will be able to, live up to all your expectations and laws.

You are always here, in all circumstances. You see the destitute and promise life after a worldly death if only they will look to you first and accept Your word as truth. You do so much that cannot be imagined or comprehended. Once and for all times, thank you.

Love, Colleen U, age 17

entire hour. In fact, I think an hour-long *adult* worship service is humanly impossible. I have trouble focusing on God alone for longer than fifteen minutes without being occasionally distracted. In fact, if someone with a bad haircut sits down in front of me in the church service, it's all over for my sense of focus!

Many churches are calling their weekend services "celebration services" or other names more accurate than "worship services." I have to concur. It's also more exact to call them "church services with worship elements" or "church services with worship moments" than "worship services."

There is no such thing as a worship *service* for children, especially if we are attempting to teach them the truth! Start simply and slowly. Allow short amounts of time (three to four minutes) for worship moments and introduce these segments in creative ways (see chapter 10).

Put the Plan in Motion

Worship takes *practice*. Repetition is the mother of skill. Repetition breeds familiarity. Familiarity breeds desire. Worship moments can be accomplished for preschool through third grade by using a simple threefold plan:

1. Say the word *worship*.
2. Deliberately shift everyone's position in the room (adds an automatic element of respect).
3. Follow immediately with something that focuses all attention on God.

One more time—

1. Say the word worship.
2. Immediately move everyone to a *different position*.
3. Direct all their attention—*focus*—toward God.

Here is an example: Everyone has been standing in the classroom, singing fun praise songs or jumping around doing hand motions. Then it's time for the worship moment. Today you have chosen a song (with words only about God) for your worship moment.

1. You say, "Now we are going to *worship* God by singing a song about Him."
2. Quietly *move* to a different position (stand, sit, kneel) or different place in the room.
3. *Sing* a song that speaks about only God.

Note: Don't use the word *worship* unless you are going to immediately focus on God!

As children hear the word *worship* and then immediately direct their attention to focusing on God, the conditioning begins. They won't initially realize what's happening. However, after a few weeks have passed, when they hear the word *worship* their brains will automatically say, "Oh, it is time for God," or "Oh, this will be something important!"

Conditioning? Sure, absolutely! It works for me!

When children grasp this concept, this looking at God, they begin responding to this closeness. This relationship with Him begins to shine in their eyes! I've seen it happen!

Worship Moment Formats

(See chapter 10 for more specific plans.)

Worship Songs

A worship song is one that talks about God, not us. Remember, this clear-cut explanation helps teach children the meaning of worship. Read the words of the songs carefully. Look for songs that don't have a lot of "me," "us," "we," "our," or "I" in them. There are "love" songs or praise songs that thank and praise God, but worship songs are about God only. A worship song allows children to sing about God without mentioning any form of self!

Worship songs describe *God* and point to *God*. For example, the song "Our God Is an Awesome God" is a familiar favorite. Music is so powerful! When singing for your worship moments, use worship songs. The following are some examples of worship songs:

"Shout to the Lord"
"Holy God, Most Holy God"
"A Mighty Fortress"
"Crown Him with Many Crowns"
"You Are Lord"
"Jesus, Name Above All Names"
"To Every Generation"
"You Are Crowned with Many Crowns"

"He Reigns"
"King of Kings"
"Celebrate Jesus"
"Blessed Be the Name of the Lord"
 "Jesus, What a Friend of Sinners"
"Holy, Holy, Holy!"
"To God Be the Glory"

Look through children's songbooks to find worship songs speaking only about God. Keep kids singing about God and who He is, and call the songs "worship songs"—over and over again.

Worship with Hands

Worshiping with hands is done to music but *without* the children singing along (see chapter 10, worship moment 2). It's worshipful choreography with arms and hands. We use a CD or tape of a worship song. The lyrics are heard, and the movements do the speaking as the children worship God. An adult leader does the hand motions in front of the class. Created motions should be written down and used consistently. The kids quietly follow the leader as the music is played.

Depending on your church background, and the "tapes" that play in your head about raising hands in worship, this may feel somewhat controversial at first. If this is an issue for you, use American Sign Language for your movements.

The word *Yadah* in the Old Testament translates "to worship with extended hands, to throw out the hands, to give thanks to God." It is obvious from verses in the Old Testament that the lifting of hands was somehow significant in worship.

Lift up your hands in the sanctuary, and bless the LORD.

Psalm 134:2 KJV

I will praise you as long as I live,
and in your name I will lift up my
hands.

Psalm 63:4

All the people lifted their hands and
responded, "Amen! Amen!"

Nehemiah 8:6

Our daughter, who is a professional choreographer, uses choreography to cement lyrics in children's minds. We use this technique for children's choirs and musical theater. One movement, consistently used for the word *God*, for example, will help them learn those particular lyrics. Choreography is an extraordinarily powerful teaching tool for worship. And children who can't easily remember words to songs or who are embarrassed to sing aloud absolutely *love* worshiping with their hands.

> Dear God,
>
> You are an awesome God. You are forgiving and patient. You are helpful because you gave us the Bible with all the answers. You give everyone a chance to get into heaven. No matter if they never go to church because they have to work or something. I love you.
>
> Love, Hannah S.,
> age 10

Worship with Dance

Dance is another effective tool to direct focus onto God. The "D word" wasn't used growing up in our home. Christians now realize that dance can be used as effectively for the Lord today as David used it in his day.

Whether it is gymnastics, ballet, or jazz, children love to express themselves through movement. Several kids we know worship God with their dance, making up choreography to worship songs. You might want to create a worship dance team. Make it a class project. Rehearse for a month, and have them perform for a worship moment.

Remind the dancers that this is not about them or their performance. It's all about God and paying attention to who

He is. Pray with them before they perform to reinforce this worship time.

They might use this dance to share God with the preschool children or other classes at church (a form of service ministry).

Worship Dramas

God invented drama. It is the most influential way to get a point across to an audience—much more effective than a sermon!

A class of fourth-grade boys was given five minutes to create a drama that would point to God. They came up with a worship drama that was shockingly effective.

One boy walked to the center of the room. He stood, holding a pile of Bibles, books, shoes, and even a couple of sweaters. One by one, his friends walked up to him and took something away, until he had nothing left in his hands. They even took his shoes. He stood quietly for a couple of seconds, looked heavenward, and said, "Thank you, God." He went on to tell us that it doesn't matter who you are, what you have or don't have. God is powerful and loving, and He never leaves you! God is always there, and we can always talk to Him.

He reminded us what kind of God we worship! Kids teach us so much, don't they?

Remember, a worship drama must be about God—pointing children to God. Drama is one of the most powerful teaching tools! And the script is right at hand. The Bible offers the most dramatic events ever recorded. Could you imagine God saying during creation, "Hmm, [yawn] something's missing. I wonder if a little light would be better"?

Bible Stories

Bible stories aren't imaginary stories. They are real and true and far more spectacular than the ones in the movies. We all love Bible stories.

Dear God,

Thank you for how magnificent you are. You have created this whole earth. In the beginning there was you, God, and no one else. Thank you for Your word that guides and convicts of sin. Thank you that Your Son was the perfect sacrifice to save all people. You are the beginning and the end, Lord, always here in times of sorrow and rejoicing.

Thank you again. Love, Leita R., age 16

Try teaching a Bible story from God's point of view for a worship moment. One summer, while I was on break from college, I taught church school for fourth-grade girls. The ten-week lesson plan chronicled the wandering and whining of the children of Israel through the wilderness around Sinai. *Ten* weeks of whining!

I planned "manna menus," and each class I wore clothing representing a different tribe of the children of Israel. My imagination was going dry, and I was running short on ways to make the story more exciting. We all got through it, trusting the Lord for a miracle and hoping some spiritual benefit had been absorbed through it all!

Imagine how the dynamics would have changed if the wilderness experience had been presented through God's eyes. What might have been *His* point of view? You see, in our humanness, we can't comprehend the love and patience God has for His children—all of us!

Imagine the unconditional love He must have felt for the Israelites, even as they constantly complained and hurt Him. He was disappointed on a daily basis, but He never once took the pillar of fire away from them. (Had I been in His place, I would have blown it out after the first two days!)

The Father's love and patient understanding is beyond human comprehension. It is supernaturally extraordinary. How does God do this? How can He put up with us, the things we do, and the way we continually let Him down?

He never waivers in His love for us. He never ever moves away. This is what makes Him God! This is the heart of God that our kids need to see. This kind of story familiarizes them with God's faithfulness.

Tell as many Bible stories from God's viewpoint as you can, introducing kids to the heart of Almighty God, giving them a different picture each time they worship.

Worship Activities

I was invited several years ago into the fifth- and sixth-grade department at church to lead "worship" for a morning service. The kids were quite surprised that I had planned a worship time without singing. (Routines make us comfortable.)

I introduced a worship activity called "You Are." I started by announcing, "A very special guest has been invited to class today." Then I asked, "What should we all do to get ready for this guest?" (Be on our best behavior, etc.) I put a chair at the front of the room and looked toward the door. (This has to be believable.) My eyes followed as an imaginary person walked in and sat in the chair in front of the group. "Oh, He's here," I said. "I am so privileged to introduce our guest. It's God."

I cautioned the class, "God is going to be with us for the next few minutes, sitting right here on this chair."

I explained that the kids were to talk to God one at a time. Each child would take a turn saying, "You are _____ (example: my friend)." I wrote their words on a marker board as, one at a time, the kids called out who God was to them.

As we played the game, the dynamics of the body language in the room were amazing. The body language dramatically changed from the start of the game to the end.

The "cool" kids, not sure they wanted to play at first, had much different attitudes by the time we finished. They snickered a little at first as others in the room called out "You Are" things to God. You could tell the kids who had never talked to God before and those who knew the "right" things to say.

A popcorn effect started and kids began speaking out of turn. It was great listening to them talking to God!

One boy said, "You are the best math tutor." Another responded, "You are rad; You are cool" (and they weren't being silly). I heard, "You rock!" "You are awesome." They were speaking from their hearts. A girl said, "You are warm."

When everything was quiet, and the board was full of all the words they had called out, I stepped back, looked at the board, and said to the kids, "We just worshiped God!"

After a pause, I said, "This is worship, because we've been thinking about who God is and what He does. These past few minutes have all been about God, focusing on only Him."

When you do this, give the class ideas to get started—You are great, You are strong, You are forgiving. Let them copy you and then say as many as they want. Patiently stand with your back to the children. Allow time for them to catch on. Eventually, it will start moving along at a comfortable pace. Any adjective is acceptable. Obviously, there should be no silliness or playing around and no talking except what is being said to God.

When the worship activity was over, there was an unexplainable hush! I picked up my things and left the room. Apparently, their behavior was exemplary the rest of the hour. It really wasn't anything I had done, you see. Structure allows the Holy Spirit to work freely in children's hearts! They had experienced a genuine time of worship. Too many people put God in a box, limiting His miraculous power. Structure doesn't limit God!

We played this "You Are" activity in adult seminar classes I taught in Sacramento last year. A couple weeks later, a letter arrived from a gentleman in northern California. It began, "I was so excited about the You Are activity we played in your workshop, I went back and introduced it to our high school group. I know you were talking about using this primarily with elementary aged children. However, I really felt the Lord said to me, 'Take this back into the high school group and see what happens.' . . . The kids loved it, and the teachers were blown away by the worship that had taken place in the youth room that night."

Praise God. Remember, anything that focuses a child on God is worship. So whatever it takes to have worship moments, go for it!

Worship Object Lessons

A teacher took a flashlight into her classroom and turned the lights out. Their lesson was about Paul and Silas in prison (Acts 16:25). She had the class sit in a circle on the floor in the corner of the room. They all sang a worship song to God (a cappella) and then talked about what kind of God He must be for these two prisoners to have loved Him so much. They talked about how, even in their darkest hour, Paul and Silas wanted to worship God.

What things about God are so life-changing that someone would want to praise Him in the middle of pain and suffering? Prisons were dark and cold; what must it have been like for these men of God? The class just sat there in the dark and sang a worship song to God and talked about Him.

A parent called the teacher later that week and said, "I can't believe the impression the Sunday school lesson made on our daughter. She's wanted to turn the lights out before dinner and sing a worship song every night, all week long."

Once kids realize they are capable of worshiping this almighty God, you know you have opened a whole new world of expression to them.

Dear God,

You are the biggest, greatest, most wonderful God. You look down on Earth every minute and protect your children. You really care what happens at school. You have a generous heart. You want everyone in heaven someday with you. You made everyone and you don't make mistakes.

Love, Kristen D., age 9

Serious Business

By the way, worship moments with children should not be multiple choice (Would you like to worship God or play or do something else?). No, this is different from story, drama, or game time. Worshiping God demands our attention and respect. Therefore, everybody participates. Even angels worship God! "And all the angels stood around the throne and the elders and the four living creatures, and fell on their faces before the throne and worshiped God" (Rev. 7:11 NKJV).

Worship is not to be taken lightly. "King Hezekiah and his officials *ordered* the Levites to praise the LORD. . . . So they sang praises with gladness and bowed their heads and worshiped" (2 Chron. 29:30, emphasis added).

If there is a behavior problem or a child doesn't cooperate, he or she might stand outside the classroom (with an adult) so that *everyone* in the room is actively worshiping God. It doesn't take more than a couple of times, and soon every child will start wanting to be a participant. Most kids don't want to miss out on what their peers are doing.

An automatic respect for God is built into this process without kids even realizing it. At what age can this respect and awe begin? How about starting when they are in the womb? Remember when Mary entered Elizabeth's house and the baby leapt inside Elizabeth because he knew they were in the presence of God? And don't forget that the media is starting to target one-year-olds!

I know nursery workers who say the word *worship* every Sunday morning when their room is filled with babies and toddlers. Immediately, they move into a time of silence and thanking God for who He is or what He has done. These teachers perform the same ritual for a couple of minutes every week. Does this routine have an effect on the subconscious minds of their little ones? Do awe and respect become part of these toddlers' lives?

Absolutely!

Worship may happen anywhere, for any person, once it has been *learned*. When this pattern is in place, get ready—because it will change your world!

PART 3

WHY

THE BENEFITS OF WORSHIP

Be a new and different person with a fresh newness in all you do and think.

Romans 12:4 TLB

Do you ever wish you could actually see a miracle happen today? The disciples saw them, even performed them all the time, right? Well, hang on to your hats! True worship is spending time face to face with the Miracle Maker.

We worship the awesome, fearsome, superior, majestic, holy, righteous, and magnificent God. He is the only perfect, true God. We lift our eyes off ourselves and turn them on God alone. It's all about seeing who He is, not who we think He is and not how we want Him to be. It's all about seeing the true God.

When we take our eyes off ourselves, miracles happen! When our focus is taken off ourselves and directed toward God, our seemingly overwhelming problems and life situations pale before His majestic brilliance. When we actually sit in awe of God, we are transformed. We become new creations. As children learn to be in awe of God, they also will be miraculously transformed!

I'm reminded of the time Jesus walked on the water and his disciples were watching from a boat (Matt. 14:27–33). Jesus told Peter to step from the boat and "come." Peter did as Jesus said. He was actually walking on the water until he took his eyes off Jesus!

Miracles happen in *our* lives when our eyes are fixed on Him! Wait a minute—*we* reap benefits by worshiping God? Yes! Go figure!

Let's look at some obvious benefits of worship.

Worship Blesses

God *commands* us to worship Him. But when we obey, look what we get from our obedience!

When Abraham obeyed, God told him, "I will surely bless you . . . and through your offspring all nations on earth will be blessed, because you have obeyed me" (Gen. 22:17–18). Genesis 39:5 tells how the Lord blessed others because of Joseph's obedience! In Deuteronomy 11:27, God promises blessings if we obey the commands of the Lord! Psalm 24:5–6 says we are promised a blessing from God if we seek His face.

When asked what it's like to have God bless you, an eight-year-old student put it this way: "We're lucky to know God, because when He blesses you, it makes your life like you're running through a cold sprinkler on a really hot day."

Several children in my ministry have had "hot" days in their short lives. I think of Bryce, diagnosed with an inoperable brain tumor, who when asked if God blesses him, lights up the room with his smile! He starts

Dear God,

You are wonderful. You are great. You are the smartest in the world. You are loving and caring. You are the best, fantastic and good.

Love, Lindsay G.
age 9

listing all the things God blesses him with, all the while telling how much he loves God!

> Blessed are they who keep his statutes
> and seek him with all their heart.
>
> Psalm 119:2

> Blessed is the man who listens to me,
> Watching daily at my gates,
> Waiting at the posts of my doors.
> For whoever finds me, finds life,
> And obtains favor from the LORD.
>
> Proverbs 8:34–35 NKJV

> A faithful man will abound with blessings.
>
> Proverbs 28:20 NKJV

I'd like to paraphrase Solomon and say a faithful *child* will abound with blessings. What better way for a child to remain faithful than to have a worship relationship with God!

Worship Heals

> For I am the LORD who heals you.
>
> Exodus 15:26 NKJV

When David was grieving over the death of his child, as his world was crumbling beneath him, God called him to worship at His throne. David said, "LORD, I will praise you with all my heart. I will tell about all of the miracles you have done" (Ps. 9:1 NIrV).

Worship involves taking our eyes off ourselves—our hurts, disappointments, and sorrows—and putting our thoughts on God. Worshiping Him will actually begin our healing process.

Worship refocuses our attention and allows healing! Let's say you're fixing dinner. While working in the kitchen, you cut your hand. Boy, it hurts! However, at the exact moment the pain seems most excruciating, the doorbell rings. You have unexpected company.

Suddenly, where is your attention? I predict the knife wound abruptly loses your focus—trust me, I've experienced this first-hand. (No pun intended.) There is an immediate need that takes precedence over the pain. That prominent need must be taken care of first.

God tells us to worship Him *first!* What would happen in our daily lives if we were to look to God first in all things?

> How great is your goodness,
>   which you have stored up for those who fear you,
>   which you bestow in the sight of men
>   on those who take refuge in you.
>
> Psalm 31:19

Early in our marriage, my husband, Duane, worked hard to start several businesses. Within fifteen years, we owned a cabinet and finished carpentry shop, with an auto body paint company next door. We had a beautiful home (oh, the advantage of being married to a carpenter!) and a secure financial future.

Our kids were in Christian schools. We were active in a great church and working in ministry. I was writing children's musical theater. Life was wonderful.

Our world collapsed when our bookkeeper embezzled more than one hundred thousand dollars from payroll taxes owed to the federal government. During the next three turbulent years, we lost our businesses, home, property, good credit, and even our cars. The Internal Revenue Service came after us in a way I never would have dreamed possible. It was paralyzing.

Dear God,

Thanks for everything you do. Thanks for lakes and rivers. Thanks for trees and cactus. Thanks for animals and birds. You are smarter than everyone.

Love, Brandon M., age 6

When we thought things couldn't get any more devastating, representatives from the IRS changed the locks on our businesses and froze our bank accounts. I helplessly watched as they posted bright red "Seizure" notices on our home and we were given thirty days to get out.

Though the embezzler was eventually found guilty after a three-year court battle and sent to jail, the IRS demanded payback with interest. From a financial and material standpoint, we had lost everything. We moved our sofas, beds, and three kids to a four-room apartment over a store.

The emotional pain was enormous. This disaster tested our marriage and devastated my husband. It uprooted our family. I found it difficult to believe I could survive.

After the first few weeks, I actually tried to have a prayer life. My prayers consisted of petitions about *me*, asking for help in *my* life. I wanted God to keep depression from overtaking *me*. I prayed for *our* seriously wounded marriage and for *our* kids. My list consisted of *our* needs, *our* next meal, *our* survival, and on and on.

Every prayer consisted of "woe is me!" You get the picture. I was a mess, taking each day fifteen minutes at a time. I remember feeling like God had totally disappeared and was doing absolutely nothing to answer my prayers. I couldn't live like this.

My heart was never focused just on God. My prayers were not about Him at all! There wasn't any time spent in adoration. There was absolutely no praise, no worship, no thanking Him for anything.

I didn't understand worship at the time. Of course, God knew and cared immensely about what I was feeling. However, He desperately wanted me to look at Him.

> You shall therefore impress these words of mine on your heart and on your soul; and you shall bind them as a sign on your hand, and they shall be as frontals on your forehead. . . . And you shall write them on the doorposts of your house and on your gates. . . . For if you are careful to keep all this commandment which I am commanding you, to do it, to love the LORD your

God, to walk in all His ways and hold fast to Him . . . there shall no man be able to stand before you; the Lord your God shall lay the dread of you and the fear of you on all the land on which you set foot, as He has spoken to you.

Deuteronomy 11:18, 20, 22, 25 NASB

Worship comes first.

Knowing what I know now, I see that if my focus had been on Him first, had I worshiped God first through the pain, the healing process would have begun immediately.

Oh, that I could have said like David in Psalm 34:1, "I will bless the LORD at all times; His praise shall continually be in my mouth" (NKJV). And in Psalm 16:8, "I have set the LORD always before me" (NKJV). If this worship relationship had become a habit as a child, my adult life would have been different.

> Dear God,
>
> You love, protect and forgive. You created great oceans and rivers. You created all the animals. Thanks,
>
> Elliot F., age 10

Jesus taught us how to pray the familiar Lord's Prayer. I never noticed that the *first* part of the prayer is worship. The focus is on him first. "Our Father, which art in heaven, [first] Hallowed be thy name. [First] Thy kingdom come. [First] Thy will be done in earth, as it is in heaven" (Matt. 6:9–10 KJV). Then it goes on to our needs and us.

Worship is spiritual *distraction*, taking our eyes off ourselves, and it brings healing. No matter what causes the pain, we must take our focus off ourselves and look at Him.

Thankfully, God is bigger than any human tragedy. As a family, we know He is the reason we survived, and our spiritual gains far outnumber our losses. Our three kids and their spouses are in full-time ministry, and our blessings abound!

Throughout his life, as David cried out in pain, his focus always turned back to God. In Psalm 40:4 he said, "Blessed is that man who makes the LORD his trust" (NKJV).

How blessed is the person who takes his eyes off himself and worships God.

Worship Empowers

The more David worshiped during his times of struggle, the more his physical strength returned, the more confidence he had to withstand his enemies and continue in the work of God.

> Who is like the LORD our God,
> Who dwells on high?
>
> Psalm 113:5 NKJV

> I was pushed back and about to fall,
>   but the LORD helped me.
> The LORD is my strength and my song;
>   he has become my salvation.
>
> Psalm 118:13–14

We desperately need God's empowerment and strength in every area. Life is exhausting. Ministry is no exception. I come from a very strong genetic line. As I write this, my eighty-year-old mom still works as a bookkeeper. A career woman—also a great homemaker—she worked outside the home while raising three children. She also taught Sunday school; sang in choir; and played the piano and organ for church, the mission on skid row, and anywhere else she was needed.

My brother, Gary, is a husband, dad to four kids, senior pastor, serious student of the Bible, and car mechanic. He only slows down long enough to yell at the TV during football games.

My sister, Susan, is a wife, mom to four sons, homemaker, and Bible study teacher. She works with a Christian humanitarian aid organization and travels into Eastern Europe to teach Bible conferences.

We all *appear* to have an endless energy capacity for ministry. The truth is, ministry is physically, emotionally, and spiritually exhausting; and Satan loves to hit us when we are down! There are many days, in all our lives, when we are so beaten down we feel like giving up. I know many of you reading this can attest to the same feelings. Some call it burnout. At my most exhausted moments in life or ministry, if I spend time in worship, my strength returns. It is miraculous. It is truly a mystery.

In order for us to be effective teachers and leaders in children's lives, we must make ourselves constantly available to God's empowerment in our own lives. There are times when we need simply to stop everything and spend time in total focus on the God of all creation and wonders.

Job was physically and emotionally exhausted when he said to the Lord, "I know that you can do all things; no plan of yours can be thwarted" (Job 42:2). Job kept his eyes on God, and he was blessed beyond his wildest dreams. God made him prosperous again.

> He is my strength, my shield from every danger. I trusted in him, and he helped me.
>
> Psalm 28:7 TLB

> But they that wait upon the LORD shall renew their strength. They shall mount up with wings like eagles; they shall run and not be weary; they shall walk and not faint.
>
> Isaiah 40:31 TLB

> Do you not know?
>   Have you not heard?
> The LORD is the everlasting God,
>   the Creator of the ends of the earth.
> He will not grow tired or weary,
>   and his understanding no one can fathom.
> He gives strength to the weary
>   and increases the power of the weak.
> Even youths grow tired and weary,
>   and young men stumble and fall;
> but those who hope in the LORD
>   will renew their strength.
>
> Isaiah 40:28–30

Empowerment is what *God promises* if we worship Him in spirit and in truth. And God keeps His promises. Oh, that our children would learn this while they are young!

Worship Is Spiritual Protection

> Contend, O LORD, with those who contend with me;
> fight against those who fight against me.
>
> Psalm 35:1

Duane and I went to great lengths to protect our children from any kind of physical harm. We were strict. Obedience was a *big* deal to us. When we called them by name (never more than twice), they responded immediately (or wished they had).

We taught our kids to obey us before they were two years old. Honestly, this was not to make me look like "Mother of the Year" in front of all my friends. It was to protect my kids! What if they were about to run into the path of an oncoming car? We wanted immediate obedience!

One day, John, then three years old, was playing with his adventurous six-year-old brother, who encouraged him to climb onto his bedroom's second-story window ledge and jump. His target below was a bath towel Mark had innocently spread on the unforgiving cement. They both thought the towel was adequate for their game. I spotted him seconds before he jumped, and I had only one chance to stop him. If John had failed to obey my instructions immediately, his jump could have resulted in his death. Did I want him to respond immediately to my commands? Absolutely!

We also desired to protect our children emotionally. I read every book on the market about self-image, self-esteem, and unconditional love. We

Dear God,

You are the strength of the world. You are the real God. You are the creator of everything. You are love and you are always here.

Love, Jessica T.,
age 10

wanted our kids immersed in the knowledge that they were secure in our love—and in God's love! We guarded their ears and eyes, not wanting anything inappropriate to get inside their precious, impressionable minds.

As parents, grandparents, and teachers, we're determined to protect children physically and emotionally. It is even more important to protect our children *spiritually*. There are *eternal* ramifications to spiritual injury or death. Whoa! How often do we think about this?

Worship is spiritual protection.

Do we want our kids at the mercy of every false doctrine or religious fad that passes through their lives? I'm distressed to hear stories of kids who run away with spiritual gurus and join strange cults.

A young woman I know, who was raised in the church, went searching to find herself after the death of her child. After trying several "free thinking" churches, she decided there was no church with any answers, and she turned her back on God completely. If she had truly known Him, if she had experienced a genuine worship relationship with Him as a child, she wouldn't have walked away.

> Do not be carried about by all kinds of strange teachings.
>
> Hebrews 13:9

We must teach kids to *really know* God in order to help them build solid relationships with Him. We can help instill in them a protection against "the flaming arrows of the evil one" (Eph. 6:16).

Worship Delivers Peace

In John 14:27 Jesus tells us, "I am leaving you with a gift— peace of mind and heart! And the peace I give isn't fragile like the peace the world gives. So don't be troubled or afraid" (TLB).

My dear college friend Mabel was diagnosed with a liver disease in 1992. Five years ago the doctors concluded that a liver transplant within five years was her ultimate cure. The five years are up, and no match has been found.

Her zany personality was demonstrated when she recently entered the hospital for an endoscopy test. When the nurse asked if she was apprehensive, she said, "Well, let me put it this way: Whenever I have an unpleasant test to face, I say to myself, 'At least it's not that test where they put that tube down your throat to your stomach.' And now you're going to do the test where you put the tube down my throat to my stomach." She had everyone in the room laughing before the test began!

It has been years of more hospitals and medical bills than you can count. Every day it gets more difficult for her just to get out of bed, but God's peace is evident in her life. I find it *humanly* incomprehensible.

> Dear God,
>
> You are our Savior. How did you make things? How did you make dogs? Thank you for families. Thank you for dying on the cross for everyone's sins. Thank you for being the Lord everyday. Thank you for Jesus. How did you make houses?
>
> We will never let go of our love for You.
>
> Love, Jackson Lee D., age 7

In a serious moment, I asked her how she sticks to God through all this. She replied, "I loved God as a child, and even today the more I learn about Him, the more reasons there are to love Him. He graciously creates in us a desire to know Him in ways we haven't before."

She pictures Him in heaven saying, "Mabel wouldn't have believed this of Me, but look how excited she is to know it now." His peace is there for the asking.

The glue was there for Mabel.

> I will both lie down in peace, and sleep;
> For You alone, O LORD, make me dwell in safety.
>
> Psalm 4:8 NKJV

The LORD will bless His people with peace.

Psalm 29:11 NKJV

Great peace have those who love Your law.

Psalm 119:165 NKJV

My son, do not forget my law,
But let your heart keep my commands;
For length of days and long life
And peace will they add to you.

Proverbs 3:1–2 NKJV

You will keep him in perfect peace, whose mind is stayed on You. [Whose mind is stayed on God? The word *stayed* means "inhabit"—sounds like worship to me!]

Isaiah 26:3 NKJV

All your children shall be taught by the LORD, and great shall be the peace of your children.

Isaiah 54:13 NKJV

These things have I spoken to you, that in Me you may have peace. In the world you will have tribulation; but be of good cheer, I have overcome the world.

John 16:33 NKJV

How will we know to ask for His peace if we don't know Him? How will our children? A worship relationship with, and intimate knowledge of, the true God places children on a firm foundation.

Worship Ensures Purity

Call it what you will, but those who walk moment by moment in a worshiping relationship with God find it almost impossible to violate His laws.

Dear God,

You are the Bread of Life and the Living Water. You are enough for everyone and everyone who isn't born yet. You are many things we don't understand. You love everyone more than anyone else could. You are kind to wait for people to get it. You are my Savior and I'll see you someday in heaven.

Love, Lauren P., age 14

In *The Broken Hearth,* William J. Bennett writes, "Since 1960, the divorce rate has more than doubled, out-of-wedlock births have skyrocketed from one in twenty to one in three, the percentage of single-parent families has more than tripled, the number of couples cohabiting has increased more than eleven fold. In record numbers, we have seen fathers deserting their wives and children—and being permitted to do so without reproach or penalty of any kind."[1]

In a world where our children think nothing of men and women living together without being married, it seems impossible to hope we can instill purity in their minds and hearts, thus saving them tremendous pain in their future. But God says it's possible!

> Finally, brethren, whatever things are true, whatever things are noble, whatever things are just, whatever things are pure, whatever things are lovely, whatever things are of good report, if there is any virtue and if there is anything praiseworthy—meditate [think, focus, familiarize, worship] on these things.
>
> Philippians 4:8 NKJV

I do not know of one instance in which adultery, infidelity, or premarital sexual relations have proven to have anything but tragic consequences in some child's life. We all know families that have been destroyed because of a lack of sexual purity. God is not the object of focus or worship when this tragedy occurs.

Do you want your kids to remain pure? Teach them to know God. Do you want them to experience solid, God-centered marriages in their futures? Teach them to worship God! The Holy Spirit has more freedom to connect with a child who effortlessly talks to God. The Holy Spirit comes through loud and clear. My own teens called it fear, guilt, or God-consciousness. Yes, it works! Children need this worship relationship to survive the temptations that will inevitably come their way.

Author Jason Perry, who writes about the teenage years in *How Far Can You Go?* says, "Meditating upon scriptures that speak of God's holiness and His demand for our holiness is one of the first steps for developing purity in our own lives."[2]

This meditating upon Scriptures doesn't happen without a preestablished worship relationship with God.

In Luke 22:40 Jesus tells His disciples a sure-fire way of not entering into temptation. He says, "Pray"! Talk to God! Worship God! Focus on God! Spend your time getting to know God and stay out of trouble!

Thirty years in ministry have caused me to witness the heartbreaking disillusionment connected with human failures. Sin takes a toll on God's earthly servants—daily. Some of the wisest advice my parents gave us as children growing up was, "Keep your eyes on God, not man. Christian men and women are human and will fail you." Churches will split, unkind words will be said, hearts will be broken, and sin will happen—yes, even with Christians.

There, but for the grace of God, go you and I and our children. Our focus must remain on Him!

Do we desire that our kids have lives full of the blessings, healing, empowerment, spiritual protection, peace, purity, and so much more that God makes available to us?

Watch what happens when a child knows God.

52 WORSHIP MOMENTS

Worship moments can happen anytime and anywhere! Say the word *worship*, change positions, and focus all conversation and adoration on God—pointing at His attributes and creation; looking at who He is, what He does, and why He came; and thanking Him with all our hearts.

Get organized! Write on your weekly schedule exactly which worship materials you will use for your worship moments. If you don't schedule a specific time, it won't happen. If you time your worship moments at home, it will be easier to incorporate your plan in class. Even if it's only three minutes a week, you are teaching kids to focus on God, and *that* is authentic scriptural worship!

Always remember that, as church teachers, we have the opportunity to touch children's live for eternity when we are only with them one hour a week. Give children the opportunity to experience the spiritual glue that will guarantee their lifelong walk with God!

1. Worship with Singing

> Worship the LORD with gladness;
> come before him with joyful songs.
>
> Psalm 100:2

Materials Needed

- Tape player or CD player
- Chalkboard or marker board (or a large piece of paper taped to the wall that all children can see)
- A worship song (suggestion: "Our God Is an Awesome God")

Step 1

Say, "Now let's *worship* God," or "This is our time to *worship* God."

Step 2

Change position: Move to a different position or place in the room. (Wait for quiet.)

Step 3

1. Ask the kids to listen carefully to the words as they sing.
2. After singing the song one or two times, ask what they heard about God—perhaps something new they learned, or something about Him they had forgotten or hadn't thought of in a while.
3. Write these points down on the board or piece of paper.
4. Sing the same song again, telling the children to think about the things they have just mentioned.

2. Worship with Hands

> I will praise you as long as I live,
>   and in your name I will lift up my hands.
>
>   Psalm 63:4

Materials Needed

- Tape player or CD player
- Worship song *with* vocals (Remember, worship songs are to be only about God.)
- Worship choreographer (leader who stands in front as music is played) who has prepared motions for this song

Step 1

Say, "Now let's *worship* God," or "This is our time to *worship* God."

Step 2

Change position: Move to a different position or place in the room. (Wait for quiet.)

Step 3

1. Play a recording of a worship song *with* vocals.
2. Explain to the kids that no one sings with the recording (even if they know the song). They are to use their *hands* to worship God.
3. The worship leader talks about using hands and arms for God. (There may be some motions that the leader wants to teach the kids before the song begins. Create the hand motions yourself or use American Sign Language. Make sure the motions are written down so they are consistent the next time this song is used.)

4. The worship leader stands in front as the song plays, leading with hand and arm choreography. The kids follow along with the worship leader.

5. Ask the children what they suppose God thought about this gift to Him.

6. Repeat the worship again if you believe the children need one more opportunity to respond to what has been discussed.

3. Worship with Dance!

> Let them praise his name with dancing.
>
> Psalm 149:3

Materials Needed

- Tape player or CD player (musical accompaniment of some sort)
- Worship songs (Remember, they are only about God.)
- Several kids to learn a worship dance number to perform for a worship moment. (Allow a week or two in advance for preparation and rehearsals.) Use this opportunity to teach children that when we do anything for God, we strive for excellence, because He always gives us His best. Caution the participants that this is not a performance—they are worshiping God, and it is best if they don't look at the children in the audience. They can imagine looking at God. Pray with participants before class; focus on this being an offering of their time and talents to God.
- A "stage" area big enough to accommodate all the children who will dance and situated so that all the children observing can see easily.

Step 1

Say, "Now let's *worship* God," or "This is our time to *worship* God."

Step 2

Change position: Move to a different position or place in the room. (Wait for quiet.)

Step 3

1. Read a Scripture verse that speaks of dancing for the Lord.

   Psalm 150:4: "Praise him with tambourine and dancing."
   Ecclesiastes 3:4: ". . . a time to weep and a time to laugh, a time to mourn and a time to dance."
   Psalm 30:11: "You turned my wailing into dancing."

2. Explain that when we worship the Lord through dance, we have an audience of *one*. We should dance for God's pleasure as we focus on Him.
3. Have the children who practiced the worship dance number present it.
4. A worship dance can also be used as a ministry to various departments or classes in the church on other occasions.

4. Worship through Drama

These commandments that I give you today are to be upon your hearts. Impress them on your children.

Deuteronomy 6:6–7

Materials Needed

Option 1

- Script (A sample follows as part of this exercise.) Use dramas that focus on *God*.
- Speaking cast (who have learned their lines ahead of time)
- All necessary props and set pieces accumulated

Option 2

- Improvisations (situations acted out on the spot). Teach the children that improvisation can be worship. The scene should make everyone focus on an aspect of God. Improvisation works wonderfully with older kids. Have kids think of situations that speak only of God or cause them to think only of God. Examples of improvisations: (1) Have a child be one of the kids who just walked across the Red Sea, dramatically telling how powerful God is to have divided the waters. (2) Have a child be one of the five thousand, trying to explain about the lunch they had on the hillside and how Jesus performed the miracle.
- Several Bible costumes

Step 1

Say, "Now let's *worship* God," or "This is our time to *worship* God."

Step 2

Change position: Move to a different position or place in the room. (Wait for quiet.)

Step 3

Option 1: Worship Drama

What's Worship?

Cast: three older elementary kids (or teens)

Props: three chairs, one table, one of the kids' shoes (or a marble or toy taken from a pocket of one of the actors)

Preparation time: two weeks. The script must be totally memorized and performed seriously for it to point to God.

Scene opens with #1 pulling #2 and #3 into room to center stage to sit on chairs (facing audience)

#1   (Pulling others) Come on, you guys, please. I want to show you something! Come on; just do this for me, okay?

#2   Okay, okay, okay . . .

#3   I'm coming, I'm coming, but I only have a couple minutes . . .

#1   This will only take a couple minutes; I promise. . . . Now just sit down facing the table here.

#2   (Sitting) All right! So . . . What? WHAT?

#3   I thought you were working on your Bible lesson. Why are we in here . . . sitting behind this table?

#1   (Excited) I AM working on my lesson on worship—and I just figured out HOW to explain it to everyone!

#2   Explain WHAT?

#1   WORSHIP! I can explain how to REALLY WORSHIP!

#3   (Already bored, yawning) I . . .uh . . . I . . . (starting to get up) you guys go on without me, I have other . . .

#1   (Pushing #3 back into chair) Oh, stop it. . . . Just go along with me for a couple minutes. . . . Okay?

#2   Okay . . . we'll do this with you; just hurry up with it.

#3   (Big sigh) Okay . . . I'll do this, but only for . . . candy.

#1 (Gives #3 dirty look; pauses) Okay . . . I'll give you some candy later. . . . Now just listen. (Suddenly looks around for something to put on the table) Let's see here . . . I need something for you guys to stare at . . . and focus on . . . (decides to take off own shoe—or pull something from pocket) I guess I can use this. (Puts shoe on table in front of friends)

#3 (Dramatically gags and falls to floor pretending the shoe smells) Aggggggggggg!

#1 (Waits until #3 has gotten laugh) Come on, you said you'd do this!

#3 (Settles down and sits back in chair) Just kidding, just kidding. . . . So . . . What do we do with the shoe?

#1 I want you both to put everything out of your minds and thoughts . . . and just focus on the shoe. Think of nothing but my shoe. Learn all you can about my shoe!

#2 (Looking at #1, thinking CRAZY!) Is there going to be a test?

#3 Is there going to be a prize?

#1 JUST DO IT! I know, I know, it sounds weird . . . but just do it . . . come on . . . please.

#3 We're supposed to stare at your shoe and focus on your shoe . . . and think only about YOUR SHOE?

#1 EXACTLY! And I'm going to time you . . . (Looking at watch) . . . because I don't think either of you can do this!

#2 (Suddenly gets a competitive look) Well, I know I can do it! But I think you're right about whozit here (Looking at #3). I doubt if FOCUS on ANYTHING is possible!

#3 (Laughing) Oh yeah? Watch this! I can focus better than YOU!

#1 (Timing) Okay . . . Ready? Now, remember . . . The rules are . . . look at the shoe, don't think of anything else. FOCUS only on the shoe . . . and think of everything you can that describes the shoe . . . got it?

#3   (Breaks focus for a second) Wait a minute. . . . You never said anything about thinking of everything you could to describe the shoe!

#2   Yeah!

#1   Oh, sorry. But you see, our minds WANDER. . . . So if we are REALLY going to focus on something . . . we need to think about that something on PURPOSE . . . so our minds don't wander around all over the place!

#2   (Pointing and laughing at #3) Yeah . . . the mind wanderer expert!

#3   (About to push #2) Hey!

#1   (Interrupts) CAN WE PLEASE DO THIS?

(Both settle down.)

#1   Okay . . . now—look at the shoe . . . think about the shoe . . . describe the shoe in your mind . . . (Looking at watch) READY . . . START!

(20 seconds of total silence with #2 and #3 staring at shoe. THEN #3 falls off chair onto floor with loud agonizing sigh.)

#3   Aggggggggggggg. I can't do it anymore . . . I can't do it anymore!

#1   (Very pleased with experiment) Great job, you guys! Great! You lasted for almost half a minute!

#3   (Getting up, shocked it wasn't very long) What? That was only thirty seconds? It felt like ten minutes!

#2   (Laughing at #3) I told you!

#1   (Still excited) No, you did GREAT . . . really, both of you, and the experiment really worked!

(#2 and #3 looking puzzled)

#2   How did it work?

#1   Well, did you focus on the shoe?

#1 and #2   Yeah.

#1   Did you block everything else out of your mind, EVERYTHING, and think only about the shoe?

#1 and #2   Yeah.

#1   Then, IT WORKED! It is possible for kids to WOR-SHIP!

(Pause)

#3   (Very confused) You've totally lost me. . . . I'm thinking you're REALLY nuts now.

#1   (Laughing) I know, wait, and let me explain. (Slowly) I found out that the word WORSHIP means "God's worth." It's only about who GOD is. So to really WORSHIP GOD, we need to think about HIM only—not ourselves, not anything else in the whole world!

#3   EVER?

#2   (Pretends to push #3) Will you just LISTEN!

(All three kids grow very serious for a moment)

#1   Listen . . . Do you get it? When we worship God, we have to focus on GOD, think only about HIM, everything we can about who God is, and why He sent Jesus . . . and how much we love HIM . . . and let nothing else in our minds while we worship Him.

#2   (Very thoughtful) Wow. I never knew that.

#3   I never knew that either. I thought WORSHIP meant . . . I don't know . . . singing . . . or . . . listening to a sermon in church . . . or I guess I never knew.

#1   (Still excited) You're right! Singing can be WORSHIP if we're thinking about God! Not ourselves. If the words we sing in the song point to GOD. Listening to a sermon can be worship if we're really focusing on God!

#2   (Looking at #3) Did you hear that? That means NOT passing notes!

#3   Yeah, yeah.

#1   It takes concentration to really WORSHIP God. And you both just proved you could focus on something COM-PLETELY, putting everything else out of your mind.

#2   Wow . . . this is really a cool way to explain worship.

#1   (Big smile) Wanna try it?

#3   What?

#1 You want to WORSHIP GOD with me for a few minutes?

#2 (Seriously) Yeah . . . I'd like to try it.

#1 (Getting up to leave) Come on, let's go get our Bibles and focus on God for a few minutes. . . .

(#2 and #3 following)

#3 (Right before exiting) Hey! When do I get my candy?

(All exit.)

Option 2: Improvisation

5. Worship like Paul in Prison

About midnight Paul and Silas were praying and singing hymns to God, and the other prisoners were listening to them.

Acts 16:25

Materials Needed

• A flashlight and dark room

Step 1

Say, "Now let's *worship* God," or "This is our time to *worship* God."

Step 2

Change position: Move to a different room that has been prepared and is dark or to a different place in the same room and turn out the lights. (Wait for quiet.)

<u>Step 3</u>

1. Read Acts 16:20–34.
2. Some background: Tell about the ministry of Paul and Silas and why they were in Philippi. Explain that these were dangerous times for anyone to stand up for Jesus and that Paul had already had repeated beatings for his belief in God. The night Paul and Silas were thrown in jail, they were stripped and beaten. Depending on the time of the year, the prisons were either cold and damp or suffocatingly hot, and they were very dirty. Paul and Silas may have gone without food. How Paul and Silas must have loved God! They worshiped Him in prison! Their God must be very important to them.
3. Have the kids suggest why Paul and Silas loved God so much.
4. Talk about the same God who is important to us. *Focus on God.*

6. Worship with God's Names—The "You Are" Activity

He will be great and will be called the Son of the Most High.

Luke 1:32

<u>Materials Needed</u>

- One chair
- Chalkboard, white board, or large pieces of paper taped to the wall on which to write
- Chalk, white-board markers, or marking pen for the paper

<u>Step 1</u>

Say, "Now let's *worship* God," or "This is our time to *worship* God."

Step 2

Change position: Move to a different position or place in the room. (Wait for quiet.)

Step 3

1. Explain that God is visiting the class today. Place a chair for God at the front of the room where all can see.
2. Explain the exercise.
3. Take turns going around the room calling out, "You are_____," using words to describe God. Give examples to help them understand and get started ("You are my friend," "You are the Creator," or other names they have learned from memory verses).
4. Stand with your back to the kids, writing their words on the board as they call them out. Be patient; let the children call out several words if they want.
5. When they are finished, look at the words together. Remind them they just worshiped God. Whenever all focus is on God, it's worship!

7. Worship: Learning God's Heart for His People

The LORD your God has blessed you in all the work of your hands. He has watched over your journey through this vast desert. These forty years the LORD your God has been with you, and you have not lacked anything.

Deuteronomy 2:7

Materials Needed

- A Bible story told through God's eyes
- A Scripture portion (an example follows)

Step 1

Say, "Now let's *worship* God," or " This is our time to *worship* God."

Step 2

Change position: Move to a different position or place in the room. (Wait for quiet.)

Step 3

1. Teach a Bible story from God's point of view. (Example: Numbers 11:4–9, 18. Once again the children of Israel were whining and complaining in the wilderness. They didn't like what they had to eat. God had saved them from being slaves in Egypt, but all they did was feel sorry for themselves.)
2. Ask the kids what they would do to the complainers if they were in God's shoes.
3. Talk about how patient and loving God was to His people. (They wanted meat and God gave them meat.)
4. Parallel it to our lives, when we feel like complaining today. Is God the same patient and loving God to us? The focus is God's heart.

8. Worship with Pictures

> Come and see what God has done,
> how awesome his works in man's behalf!
>
> Psalm 66:5

Materials Needed

- Magazines (to be cut up)

Step 1

Say, "Now let's *worship* God," or "This is our time to *worship* God."

Step 2

Change position: Move to a different position or place in the room. (Wait for quiet.)

Step 3

1. Have the children cut out one or two pictures from magazines—anything that might show the nature, or character, of God. As long as the assignment is taken seriously, children can use any pictures they want.
2. Have the children take turns explaining how each picture points to God.

9. Worship: Look at the Heavens!

> When I consider your heavens,
>   the work of your fingers,
> the moon and the stars,
>   which you have set in place, . . .
>   how majestic is your name in all the earth!
>
> Psalm 8:3, 9

Materials Needed

- Glow-in-the-dark sun, moon, and stars (found in party supply stores). Stick them to the ceiling in the classroom.

Step 1

Say, "Now let's *worship* God," or "This is our time to *worship* God."

Step 2

Change position: Have the children lie on their backs on the floor. Turn out the lights and wait for quiet.

Step 3

1. Point out the stars and moon and talk about the Creator.
2. Name as many heavenly bodies as you can. Name stars and constellations. Try to get them to grasp the concept of trillions of stars and the unending universe. Depending on the children's age, speak about light year statistics.

Impress upon them that God, not George Lucas, created all this. Tell the information with an awe and wonder in your voice, and let them sense His magnificent creation as they gaze at the ceiling.

10. Worship: God Gives Peace

Peace I leave you; my peace I give you.

John 14:27

Materials Needed

- Invite a guest from the congregation who has gone through something sad. Have them tell the kids how God is the Comforter and gives us peace. Explain how in their own strength they couldn't have made it through the pain, how they couldn't have survived without God's peace. (Caution: This worship moment could easily bring the focus on the individual speaking, so be sure that they understand the purpose of the worship moment. We are to learn about God's peace.)

Step 1

Say, "Now let's *worship* God," or "This is our time to *worship* God."

Step 2

Change position: Move to a different position or place in the room. (Wait for quiet.)

Step 3

1. Introduce the guest speaker, setting the tone for the worship moment by reading a verse that explains the subject/purpose. (For example, Isaiah 26:3: "You will keep in perfect peace him whose mind is steadfast, because he trusts in you.")
2. After the speaker gives a brief testimony, refocus the children on the attributes of God, then quickly sum up. Remind them of the need to focus on God.

11. Worship: God Heals

Jesus went through all the towns and villages . . . healing every disease and sickness.

Matthew 9:35

He heals the brokenhearted
and binds up their wounds.

Psalm 147:3

He welcomed them and spoke to them about the kingdom of God, and healed those who needed healing.

Luke 9:11

Materials Needed

- Large piece(s) of paper taped to the wall
- Marking pen for paper

Step 1

Say, "Now let's *worship* God," or "This is our time to *worship* God."

Step 2

Change position: Move to a different position or place in the room. (Wait for quiet.)

Step 3

1. Have a number of the children share their own stories, showing sore knees, cuts, and bruises (short versions).
2. Write all the visible injuries on a piece of paper that will be kept until the next week.
3. Tell the children, "Next week we'll see how God made our bodies to heal each sore." Talk about God the Healer. Focus on God's power of healing!

12. Special "God-Created" Guest

Like newborn babies, crave pure spiritual milk, so that by it you may grow up in your salvation.

1 Peter 2:2

For you created my inmost being;
you knit me together in my mother's womb.
I praise you because I am fearfully and wonderfully made.

Psalm 139:13–14

Materials Needed

- A newborn baby to visit the class for a couple minutes

Step 1

Say, "Now let's *worship* God," or "This is our time to *worship* God."

Step 2

Change position: Move to a different position or place in the room. (Wait for quiet.)

Step 3

Option 1

1. Ask what God means when he says we should be like babies, wanting to eat (learn) all the time from God's Word.
2. Ask what happens if a baby does not eat right—and what happens to a Christian who doesn't continue to learn more about God.
3. Talk about food that babies eat to grow strong—how does *really* knowing God make us stronger?

_____Option 2

1. Look at the little fingers and toes, etc.; talk about the fact that only God can create life. With all of the inventions in the world, science has yet to create from nothing.
2. Come prepared with some impressive statistics (how many veins are in the baby's body, how big the heart is, etc.—something to make the kids react in awe) and talk about the Creator.
3. Remind them that God knows how many hairs we have on our heads (Matt. 10:30) and that He continues to know *everything* about us, not just what we were like before we were born.

Be prepared for questions about children born with disabilities. Did God make them that way?

13. Worship: God Uses Sounds

Let the sea resound. . . .

Psalm 96:11

His lightning lights up the world;
the earth sees and trembles.

Psalm 97:4

Let the rivers clap their hands.

Psalm 98:8

Materials Needed

- Sound effects recording (There are many kinds of sound effects tapes . . . nature sounds, water, rain, thunder, etc.)
- Tape recorder

Step 1

Say, "Now let's *worship* God," or "This is our time to *worship* God."

Step 2

Change position: Move to a different position or place in the room. (Wait for quiet.)

Step 3

1. Play one of the sound effects.
2. Talk about the Creator.
3. Read Scriptures that tell about each particular sound.

   Examples:
   Exodus 19:16—thunder and lightning
   Revelation 8—earthquakes
   2 Kings 7—noise of horses
   Ezekiel 1—noise of wings
   Joel 2—noise of a flame and fire

14. Worship with Nature

Then God said, "Let the land produce vegetation: seed-bearing plants and trees on the land that bear fruit with seed in it. . . ." And it was so.

Genesis 1:11

Materials Needed

- Bird seed (or flower seeds)
- Flower pots (one for each child, or one or two for the room)
- Potting soil
- Optional: large piece of paper taped to the wall

Step 1

Say, "Now let's *worship* God," or "This is our time to *worship* God."

Step 2

Change position: Move to a different position or place in the room. (If the kids are going to plant the seeds, then you might want them to finish all the planting before moving to a location where the pots can be seen as you speak.)

Step 3

1. Plant seeds in a pot to watch them sprout over the next few weeks.
2. Talk about the Creator of the flowers and trees and all growing things.
3. List (speaking or writing down) some names of flowers or plants God created.
4. Talk about the various colors and sizes and shapes.
5. Tell about the different foliage for different parts of the earth. List amazing information about what God has created.

15. Worship: Take a Walk!

. . . that I may walk before the Lord in the land of the living.

Psalm 116:9

Materials Needed

- Before class begins, send a note to inform parents about the walk.
- A planned route where children can go with the least amount of disturbance to other classes. Walk the route

ahead of time. See it through the eyes of a child so you know what to expect and whether or not the route will serve your purpose for the worship moment.

Step 1

Say, "Now let's *worship* God," or "This is our time to *worship* God."

Step 2

Change position: Leave the classroom for a few minutes.

Step 3

When outside (after waiting for quiet)
1. Tell the children to find one "piece" of God's creation, bring it back to the classroom with them, and tell why they think God might have created it.
2. As different children share, be prepared to read verses mentioning each creation. Older kids could be given the references and asked to find examples.

> Leaves—Mark 11:13
> Rock—Job 30:6
> Dirt (or dust)—Psalm 18:42
> Flower—1 Kings 6:29
> Branch (or vine)—John 15:4
> Water or vegetables—Daniel 1:12
> Wood—Genesis 6:14
> Worm—Isaiah 51:8

16. Worship the God of Miracles

Many people saw the miraculous signs he was doing and believed in his name.

John 2:23

Materials Needed

- Bible story video clips
- TV and VCR

Step 1

Say, "Now let's *worship* God," or "This is our time to *worship* God."

Step 2

Change position: Move to a different position or place in the room. (Wait for quiet.)

Step 3

1. Pick a clip of a miracle from a Bible story video (*The Jesus Film,* for example) and play it.
2. Talk about God's miracles and how we worship the same God today who did those miracles long ago. Read the Scripture reference relating to each miracle.
3. Think about the miracles that God does now (creation of life, salvation).

17. Worship with the Scriptures

In reading this, then, you will be able to understand my insight into the mystery of Christ.

Ephesians 3:4

Materials Needed

- A Bible for each child

Step 1

Say, "Now let's *worship* God," or "This is our time to *worship* God."

Step 2

Change position: Move to a different position or place in the room. (Wait for quiet.)

Step 3

1. Read together slowly, with lots of expression, a passage of Scripture that points to, or talks only about, God. Psalm 93 works well:

    > The LORD reigns, he is robed in majesty;
    >   the LORD is robed in majesty
    >   and is armed with strength.
    > The world is firmly established,
    >   it cannot be moved.
    > Your throne was established long ago;
    >   you are from all eternity.
    >
    > The seas have lifted up, O LORD,
    >   the seas have lifted up their voice;
    >   the seas have lifted up their pounding waves.
    > Mightier than the thunder of the great waters,
    >   mightier than the breakers of the sea—
    >   the LORD on high is mighty.
    >
    > Your statutes stand firm;
    >   holiness adorns your house
    >   for endless days, O LORD.

2. Depending on the children's age, this worship moment may only need a period of reflective silence after the reading of the verses. Older kids may take a sentence from this

passage and give examples of what we see in the world today (e.g., hurricanes, tornados, etc.)

18. Worship: "Take-Home" Research

> Your name, O LORD, endures forever,
>   your renown, O LORD, through all generations.
>
> Psalm 135:13

Materials Needed

- A Bible for each child
- Optional: a small writing tablet they could continue to use after this specific assignment is over

Step 1

Say, "Now let's *worship* God," or "This is our time to *worship* God."

Step 2

Change position: Move to a different position or place in the room. (Wait for quiet.)

Step 3

1. Talk about Psalm 135:13, explaining that the more things we know about God, the easier it is to remember Him as He instructs us in His Word. We worship as we remember everything we can about God.
2. Assign research in the Book of Psalms. Tell the children to write down every attribute about God they can find. They are to come next week with their lists. How much can they remember without looking at their list? Promise

a treat for everyone who does the assignment. (Rewards work too!)

19. Worship: More Research

Children, obey your parents in the LORD, for this is right.

Ephesians 6:1

Materials Needed

- A Bible for each child
- Optional: a small writing tablet they could continue to use after this specific assignment is over

Step 1

Say, "Now let's *worship* God," or "This is our time to *worship* God."

Step 2

Change position: Move to a different position or place in the room. (Wait for quiet.)

Step 3

1. Read Ephesians 6:1, explaining that our deeds (things we do physically) can also cause us to focus on God.
2. Ask the children to write down things this week that they did because they wanted to please God (worshiping Him in the process). Examples:

Obeying parents (We obey because God wants us to and it pleases Him.)
Doing chores even if we don't feel like it because we know it pleases God

Being nice
Sharing with our siblings
Other attributes our parents expect and which we
know will please God

20. Worship: Thirsty for God!

Blessed are those who do hunger and thirst for righteousness, for they will be filled.

Matthew 5:6

Option 1

Materials Needed

- Potato chips
- Glasses of water where they can be seen but not reached

Put chips out for everyone to eat when they first arrive. When they continually ask for a drink:

Step 1

Say, "Let's have our *worship* time."

Step 2

Change position (the teacher). Wait for quiet.

Step 3

1. Open by asking for an explanation of how they might feel (thirsty).
2. Read Matthew 5:6, explaining that God wants us to be that thirsty for Him and His Word.

3. Give the children the water.
4. Explain that their thirst being "quenched," their being satisfied, is just what God will do in our hearts and lives when we read His Word and pray. He satisfies our hearts.

Option 2

Materials Needed

- Birthday cake
- Optional: birthday decorations

Set up the classroom for a birthday party. As the class begins, ignore questions as to why there is a birthday cake in the room. Read Matthew 5:6.

Teach the same principle, saying, "God wants us to hunger after righteousness more than anything else!"

21. Worship with Imagination

But when you pray, go into your room.

Matthew 6:6

Materials Needed

- Imaginary isolation booth
- Something to represent an imaginary isolation booth for each child to take home for the week (We gave each child a bookmark with a verse on prayer, but anything tangible will do—so that when they see it, they will be reminded to do this exercise.)

Step 1

Say, "Now let's *worship* God," or "This is our time to *worship* God."

Step 2

Change position: Move to a different position or place in the room. (Wait for quiet.)

Step 3

1. Talk about prayer—how it is more than just talking to God about the things we want, but it is first about Him.
2. Remind them that worship takes place anywhere—not just at church.
3. Tell them that this week everyone is going to take home a special "isolation booth"/prayer and praise closet.
4. Ask for their suggestions as to where they could keep it at home (in the closet, etc.).
5. Tell them to go into their isolation booth every day this week for some worship time with God.

22. Worship and Art I

In the beginning God created . . .

Genesis 1:1

Materials Needed

Option 1

• Clay

Option 2

- Paper
- Crayons

Step 1

Say, "Now let's *worship* God," or "This is our time to *worship* God."

Step 2

Change position: Move to a different position or place in the room. (Wait for quiet.)

Step 3

1. Give children a lump of clay or paper and crayons, and allow three to five minutes for them to form something they know God made.
2. Talk about why He might have made such a thing. Mention Genesis 1:11–12. This is also a wonderful opportunity to teach that only God can create (form something from nothing)! Humans have been discovering, making, and designing, but only God can create.

To learn the heart of God sets the foundation to know God.

23. Worship and Art II

Have you entered the storehouses of the snow?

Job 38:22

Materials Needed

* White paper and scissors for every child

Step 1

Say, "Now let's *worship* God," or "This is our time to *worship* God."

Step 2

Change position: Move to a different position or place in the room. (Wait for quiet.)

Step 3

1. Show the children how to fold and cut their papers to make snowflakes.
2. Discuss what God might have been thinking when He created snow. (There are no right or wrong answers; this is speculation.) Help them *see* the mind and heart and imagination of our incredibly complicated God.
3. Tell about snowflake designs—how every flake that falls to the ground has its own unique design. There are no two alike—just like there are no two people alike!
4. Hang the snowflakes around the room for a couple of weeks to be a reminder of the Creator.

The art exercises are worship moments, so the children need to do the art projects quietly, *thinking* about how God created things.

24. Worship in Writing

Give thanks unto the LORD, for he is good.

1 Chronicles 16:34

Materials Needed

- Thank-you notes
- Pencils or pens for every child

Step 1

Say, "Now let's *worship* God," or "This is our time to *worship* God."

Step 2

Change position: Move to a different position or place in the room. (Wait for quiet.)

Step 3

1. Have each child write God a thank-you note, thanking Him for who He is and what He has done. Instruct the children that these are not to be about us, only God. (This activity might take longer than anticipated; notes may have to be rewritten until they understand.)
2. Have a few of the kids read their cards aloud.
3. Put the cards up around the room to be a reminder of all we have to be thankful for.

25. Worship and Forgiveness I

If we confess our sins, he is faithful and just and will forgive us our sins and purify us from all unrighteousness.

1 John 1:9

Materials Needed

- Soap
- A really dirty object or a piece of fabric

- Something that will make the object even dirtier (for example, dirt!)
- Spot remover

Note: Try this exercise at home before presenting it to the children.

Step 1

Say, "Now let's *worship* God," or "This is our time to *worship* God."

Step 2

Change position: Move to a different position or place in the room. (Wait for quiet.)

Step 3

1. With the dirty object in your hands (or in front of you), talk about sin as you make the object even dirtier.
2. Take the spot remover and wash away the dirt.
3. Talk about how Jesus' death on the cross provided a way to wash "my" sin and "your" sin away—not just the sins of the world. And God cleans our lives—washes us white as snow. He doesn't just cover it up or overlook it! Talk about God's grace (we don't do anything to deserve this) and His forgiveness because of His unconditional love (1 John 1:8–9). Bring the focus back to God.

26. Worship and Forgiveness II

Be kind and compassionate to one another, forgiving each other, just as in Christ God forgave you.

Ephesians 4:32

Materials Needed

- Magic paper (Purchase this at a magic store.)
- Pencils
- Matches
- Empty coffee can
- Safety precautions: potholder and water nearby

Step 1

Say, "Now let's *worship* God," or "This is our time to *worship* God."

Step 2

Change position: Move to a different position or place in the room. (Wait for quiet.)

Step 3

1. Pass out a piece of magic paper to the children, having each one write his or her worst sin on the paper.
2. Collect the papers and put them in an empty coffee can.
3. Throw a lit match in with the papers. When the fire is gone, the papers will have all burned up, but if you turn the can upside down (remember to use the potholder) . . . nothing comes out! Every ash has disappeared! This is such a great example of God's total forgiveness! (John 3:16). Focus on a forgiving God.

27. Worship and Miracles

Receive your sight; your faith has healed you.

Luke 18:42

Materials Needed

- Blindfolds (Use strips of cloth.)

Step 1

Say, "Now let's *worship* God," or "This is our time to *worship* God."

Step 2

Change position: Move to a different position or place in the room. (Wait for quiet.)

Step 3

1. Have every child put on a blindfold. Tell them to leave them on (for two or three minutes) but to walk around the room and talk with their friends. You might have small tasks they could do (pick up papers, books, etc.) Make sure there is nothing around with which they could really hurt themselves.
2. After the students have gotten a small taste of what a blind man might have experienced, have them remove the blindfolds.
3. Ask them how they felt (awkward, scared, helpless?).
4. Talk about God the Healer and the miracles He had His Son perform on earth. Use this opportunity to ask the kids why God might perform miracles today. The focus is God's power.

28. Worship and Drama (David for a Day)

> But I trust in you, O LORD; I say, "You are my God."
>
> Psalm 31:14

Materials Needed

- Bibles for kids to take turns reading
- One prop for each of the following scenarios:

  David as the shepherd boy fighting lions—1 Samuel
  17:34–37 (shepherd's staff)
  David fighting Goliath—1 Samuel 17:40–49 (sling)
  David fighting the Philistines—1 Samuel 23:4–5
  (sword)
  David crowned king—2 Samuel 5:1–4 (crown)

Step 1

Say, "Now let's *worship* God," or "This is our time to *worship* God."

Step 2

Change position: Move to a different position or place in the room. (Wait for quiet.)

Step 3

1. Talk a little bit about the life of David, reminding the students of all that God did for him in various circumstances. God called him His beloved.
2. Have each of the children pretend they are David for a few minutes.
3. Read a verse where David expresses his praise to God for something in particular. Try to get each child to find something different. (With a little help from the teacher, this is so powerful!) Examples:

   Psalm 23—shepherd
   Psalm 25—guidance
   Psalm 30—deliverance from death

Psalm 34—provider

Psalm 65—thanking God for the beautiful creation

4. If the students are older, challenge them to take some time to pretend they are David for a week and have them write down what they discover in Psalms during the week. Use the worship time the following Sunday to have them share their findings.

29. Worship and God's Attributes

So in Christ we who are many form one body, and each member belongs to all the others.

Romans 12:5

Materials Needed

• None

Step 1

Say, "Now let's *worship* God," or "This is our time to *worship* God."

Step 2

Change position: Move to a different position or place in the room. (Wait for quiet.)

Step 3

1. Today, everyone will switch identities with another person (child or teacher) in the room.
2. Everyone is to ask the person they want to be what they love about God today.

3. Take turns sharing that special thought about God with the group as if you were the other person. (Suzie becomes Carol for a day; she loves God because He made the ocean and she loves to go to the beach. Bobby becomes Tom and loves that God gave him a baby brother, etc.)

30. Worship and Our Love for God

Ascribe to the LORD the glory due his name;
worship the LORD in the splendor of his holiness.

Psalm 29:2

Materials Needed

- A large poster board or pieces of paper taped to the wall on which you can write
- Large marking pen

Step 1

Say, "Now let's *worship* God," or "This is our time to *worship* God."

Step 2

Change position: Move to a different position or place in the room. (Wait for quiet.)

Step 3

1. For three or four weeks, write one or two things on the poster board/paper that you love about God.
2. Read a verse in the Bible that mentions these qualities. (Example: God forgives sin—1 John 1:9)
3. Clearly define these attributes as you add them each week and relate them to the kids' lives as well as yours!

This is a great worship moment because, as you personalize these thoughts, the children know *you mean* what you teach—and that you are also still learning!

31. Worship and Music

> I will sing of your love and justice;
> to you, O LORD, I will sing praise.
>
> Psalm 101:1

Materials Needed

- Writing paper
- A familiar tune that the majority of children will know

Step 1

Say, "Now let's *worship* God," or "This is our time to *worship* God."

Step 2

Change position: Move to a different position or place in the room. (Wait for quiet.)

Step 3

1. Write a song. Take a familiar tune the kids know (even one you sing at church), and write a worship song. (Remember, no personal pronouns that refer to self!) Psalms is a great resource. See especially Psalm 147:1.
2. Sing it to God.

Here's an example:

> You are Creator, above all others.
> You made the sun and moon and stars.
> You made the oceans and all the planets,
> Amazing God, You truly are!

32. Worship and God's Creation

Through him all things were made; without him nothing was made that has been made.

John 1:3

Materials Needed

- Apples (or another fruit)—enough for everyone
- Napkins and paper plates
- A knife
- A little research on the fruit you choose to use

Step 1

Say, "Now let's *worship* God," or "This is our time to *worship* God."

Step 2

Change position: Move to a different position or place in the room. (Wait for quiet.)

Step 3

1. Cut up the fruit, looking at every part of it carefully.
2. Ask the kids what they observe.
3. Talk about it being an amazing miracle how it grows and how it knows when to stop growing!

4. Do some research on the fruit. The more interesting the facts, the more amazing God will seem to children.

> Apples have been around since before Jesus!
> There are carvings of apples on ancient tombs in the Middle East.
> The first apples in America were mainly used for cider.[1]

33. Worship and the Cross

So the soldiers took charge of Jesus. Carrying his own cross, he went out to the place of the Skull (which in Aramaic is called Golgotha). Here they crucified him, and with him two others—one on each side and Jesus in the middle.

John 19:16–18

Materials Needed

- Wood, or a large beam that would give an idea of how heavy the cross could have been
- Large nails
- Thorns

Step 1

Say, "Now let's *worship* God," or "This is our time to *worship* God."

Step 2

Change position: Move to a different position or place in the room. (Wait for quiet.)

Step 3

1. As you tell about Jesus dying on the cross, explain each object you have brought with you as it fits into the story.
2. Pass around the object explaining the hurt and pain it caused Jesus—all because of sin.
3. Explain that Jesus was crucified for us—because *He* is love.

34. Worship and Salt

You are the salt of the earth. But if the salt loses its saltiness, how can it be made salty again?

Matthew 5:13

Materials Needed

• Chunk of salt (or a salt shaker if block salt is not available)

Step 1

Say, "Now let's *worship* God," or "This is our time to *worship* God."

Step 2

Change position: Move to a different position or place in the room. (Wait for quiet.)

Step 3

1. Make sure that each child has some salt.
2. Have them taste it and then ask: How does it taste? How is it different from other tastes? What happens when you

eat a lot? (You get thirsty.) Why is our being salt important to *Him?*

Research fact: Salt is a mineral vital to life itself! It has many uses.

35. Worship and Creation

Every good and perfect gift is from above, coming down from the Father of the heavenly lights.

James 1:17

Materials Needed

- A flower for each child
- Optional: "vases" to put them in

Step 1

Say, "Now let's *worship* God," or "This is our time to *worship* God."

Step 2

Change position: Move to a different position or place in the room. (Wait for quiet.)

Step 3

1. Line up all the flowers in a row.
2. Let the children take turns describing them (the pretty colors, the different sizes, shapes, textures, smells, etc.).
3. Ask the children why they think God would make these flowers and what He might want to show to the world through such beautiful creations.

4. Share two or three Scriptures that talk about why God would make such beautiful creations (e.g., 1 Kings 6:35; Song of Sol. 2:12).

36. Worship Instruction

Worship the Lord your God, and serve him only.

Matthew 4:10

Materials Needed

- A Bible for each child

Step 1

Say, "Now let's *worship* God," or "This is our time to *worship* God."

Step 2

Change position: Move to a different position or place in the room. (Wait for quiet.)

Step 3

This exercise can be done in a variety of ways depending on the age of your students. Have everyone work together. Have the students split into groups of two or three each.

1. Have each child read a verse where the word *worship* is used in Scripture (e.g., Pss. 5:7; 22:27, 29; 29:2; 45:11; 66:4; 81:9; 86:9; 95:6; 96:9; 97:7; 99:5, 9; 132:7; 138:2).
2. Discuss how the word *worship* is used in that verse, making sure the children really understand what the verse is teaching.

Remember, worship involves study about God (learning all we can about Him, learning His heart).

37. Worship with Lent

[He] made himself nothing, taking the very nature of a servant, being made in human likeness. And being found in appearance as a man, he humbled himself and became obedient to death—even death on a cross!

Philippians 2:7–8

Note: Lent is a six-week period in the Christian calendar leading up to Easter. Many denominations use this time to remember the sacrifice Jesus made for us on the cross by purposely abstaining from some physical pleasure. Giving up chocolate or candy for this period of time is one option.

Materials Needed

- Paper
- Pencils or pens for each child

Step 1

Say, "Now let's *worship* God," or "This is our time to *worship* God."

Step 2

Change position: Move to a different position or place in the room. (Wait for quiet.)

Step 3

1. Remind the children all that Jesus gave up for them when He came to earth.

2. Discuss what Lent is for—your own time of self-sacrificing for God.
3. Every child can write on a piece of paper the one thing they won't eat (or do) for the week as a form of worship because of all Jesus gave up for us.
4. Teach them that this is not something to brag about—or tell everyone what they are giving up—Jesus humbled Himself. Make sure they also know this has nothing to do with earning salvation.

38. Worship Altar

These stones are to be a memorial to the people of Israel forever.

Joshua 4:7

Materials Needed

- A blanket or material to lay on the floor
- A rock for each child

Step 1

Say, "Now let's *worship* God," or "This is our time to *worship* God."

Step 2

Change position: Move to a different position or place in the room. (Wait for quiet.)

Step 3

1. Read Joshua 4:1–7.
2. Explain carefully why there was an altar.

3. Make a small rock altar, much like God's people might have done in the Old Testament.
4. Each time a rock is put on the altar, say one thing that we should remember about God (He is good, He protects, etc.).
5. Talk about how the people were obedient in building the altar (see also Gen. 8:20).
6. If possible, leave the altar in the classroom for a couple of weeks as a reminder.

39. Worship and the Ten Commandments

. . . but showing love to a thousand generations of those who love me and keep my commandments.

Exodus 20:6

Materials Needed

• Paper and crayons for each child

Step 1

Say, "Now let's *worship* God," or "This is our time to *worship* God."

Step 2

Change position: Move to a different position or place in the room. (Wait for quiet.)

Step 3

Option 1

1. Have the kids draw what they think the stones that God wrote the Ten Commandments on might have looked like when He gave them to Moses.
2. Then read them Exodus 20:1–17 and talk about them *from God's point of view.*

Option 2

1. Have the kids draw what they think the stones that God wrote the Ten Commandments on might have looked like when He gave them to Moses.
2. Pick one or two of the commandments to read and then have the children write those commandments on their "tablets."
3. Use this as your worship moment over the next two or three weeks, having the kids add to their tablets each week. If possible, display the tablets on the walls each week after the kids add to them.

40. Worship and God's Opinion

"For my thoughts are not your thoughts, neither are your ways my ways," declares the LORD.

Isaiah 55:8

Materials Needed

• Bibles with concordances for each child

Step 1

Say, "Now let's *worship* God," or "This is our time to *worship* God."

Step 2

Change position: Move to a different position or place in the room. (Wait for quiet.)

Step 3

1. Give each child a word (or have two or three children work on one word together). Examples: prayer, love, joy, mother, singing, darkness, heaven, lying, pride.
2. Have them look in a concordance to find a verse that tells what God has to say about it.
3. Ask each child to explain how the verse helps him or her to know how God feels about that particular word. If the first verse they look up doesn't make sense to them, encourage them to keep searching until they find one they can understand and talk about. Adults can't always explain verses either!

41. Worship and a Rainbow

I have set my rainbow in the clouds, and it will be the sign of the covenant between me and the earth.

Genesis 9:13

Materials Needed

• Chalk, paint, crayons, markers
• Large pieces of paper for each child

Step 1

Say, "Now let's *worship* God," or "This is our time to *worship* God."

Step 2

Change position: Move to a different position or place in the room. (Wait for quiet.)

Step 3

1. Have the children make a rainbow.
2. Talk about why God created the first rainbow.
3. For older children, you might want to get some "scientific" facts about light/rainbows/the curve of the earth. Wow them with the awesome imagination of God!

42. Worship with Offering

Then the LORD will have men who will bring offerings in righteousness.

Malachi 3:3

Materials Needed

• Paper and pencils

Step 1

Say, "Now let's *worship* God," or "This is our time to *worship* God."

Step 2

Change position: Move to a different position or place in the room. (Wait for quiet.)

Step 3

1. Talk about offerings. You can use examples of all the worship offerings in the Old Testament (see Leviticus 1–5).
2. Decide collectively what the class could give to God with their offerings.
3. Have each child write it down.
4. Discuss what each child could do to *earn* some money during the week in order to bring in the money the following Sunday. (There may be people in the congregation willing to "hire" the children to do jobs to increase their offering. Remind the children that God doesn't *need* our money or things; He wants us to love Him and His work so much that we *want* to give to Him!
5. If there are children who cannot earn money during the week, they may have something personal they would like to give as an offering to the Lord (stuffed animal, special book, etc.). Arrange to have those given to homeless children or children in the hospital.

43. Worship and Light

I am the light of the world. Whoever follows me will never walk in the darkness, but will have the light of life.

John 8:12

Your word is a lamp to my feet
and a light to my path.

Psalm 119:105

Materials Needed

- Flashlight
- A room that can be very dark

Step 1

Say, "Now let's *worship* God," or "This is our time to *worship* God."

Step 2

Change position: Move to a different position or place in the room. (Wait for quiet.)

Step 3

Option 1

1. Read John 8:12 (better yet—if you have it memorized, you can recite it while the room is still dark).
2. Turn on the flashlight.
3. Ask the kids why God calls Himself the light of the world. Have the kids each give an opinion.

Option 2

1. While the room is dark, read Psalm 119:105.
2. Turn on the flashlight, but keep it focused on the floor.
3. Ask the kids to explain how God's Word is a light to our path.

44. Worship and Baby Jesus

And she gave birth to her firstborn, a son. She wrapped him in cloths and placed him in a manger, because there was no room for them in the inn.

Luke 2:7

Materials Needed

- A builder or carpenter to assemble the stable (either ahead of time or as the kids watch)
- Old boards to make a small "lean-to" stable
- Dirt or straw
- Smell—as it probably was smelly at Jesus' birth (use your imagination as to how to do this!)

Step 1

Change position: Move outdoors. (Wait for quiet.)

Step 2

Say, "Now let's *worship* God," or "This is our time to *worship* God."

Step 3

1. Ask the kids to make observations about the "stable."
2. Talk about God's part in this plan and why He would send Jesus into the world in such a place.
3. For older children, this is a great opportunity to introduce them to the prophecies in the Old Testament concerning the coming of the Messiah. (See Isaiah 53.)

45. Worship as a Disciple

"Come, follow me," Jesus said, "and I will make you fishers of men."

Mark 1:17

Materials Needed

* List of Jesus' disciples (and perhaps pictures):

    Simon Peter
    Andrew
    James
    John
    Phillip
    Thomas
    Matthew
    James
    Thaddeus
    Simon
    Judas
    Bartholomew

* Character or personality descriptions (include the jobs each did)
* Paper and pencils

Step 1

Say, "Now let's *worship* God," or "This is our time to *worship* God."

Step 2

Change position: Move to a different position or place in the room. (Wait for quiet.)

Step 3

1. Read Mark 1:16–21. Briefly "introduce" each of the disciples to the kids.
2. Have the kids each pick a disciple they want to be throughout the week.
3. Remind the kids that the disciples spent hours with Jesus, listening to His teaching. Ask them how they could do this during the week (read portions of the Gospels).
4. Tell them that they are to come the next Sunday with a list of things they learned about Jesus during the week and what they love most about Jesus.
5. The following Sunday ask why the disciple they chose decided to follow Jesus.

46. Worship with Proverbs

. . . for understanding proverbs and parables, the sayings and riddles of the wise.

Proverbs 1:6

Materials Needed

• A Bible for every child

Step 1

Say, "Now let's *worship* God," or "This is our time to *worship* God."

Step 2

Change position: Move to a different position or place in the room. (Wait for quiet.)

Step 3

1. Let the kids team up in pairs and select a favorite proverb. Examples:

    Proverbs 3:3
    Proverbs 4:23
    Proverbs 6:16–19
    Proverbs 8:10
    Proverbs 9:34–35
    Proverbs 10:8
    Proverbs 10:11
    Proverbs 11:29

2. Have them explain: What does God want to teach through it? What does that show or teach us about God? (For example, He wants us to behave a certain way so that He can bless us because He is love, or He is kind, or He is all knowing and knows what would be good for us. Or, as in Proverbs 6:16–19, because He is pure and holy.)

47. Worship with Drama

I am God Almighty.

> Genesis 17:1

Materials Needed

- Several costume pieces (hats/scarves)
- Several props (a crown for a king, a staff for a shepherd, a bread wrapper for bread, flashlight for light)
  (Or send a postcard to each child in the class during the week prior asking them to bring a prop or costume into class that could depict an attribute of God.)
- Scriptures telling an attribute of God—one Scripture for every prop or costume piece

Step 1

Say, "Now let's *worship* God," or "This is our time to *worship* God."

Step 2

Change position: Move to a different position or place in the room. (Wait for quiet.)

Step 3

1. Put all the items on a table in the front of the room.
2. Read a Scripture passage. Examples:

> Genesis 1—creator
> Job 36:22—teacher
> Psalm 47:7—king
> Psalm 50:6—judge
> Psalm 78:35—rock
> Psalm 84:9—shield
> John 15—vine
> 1 John 1:5—light

3. Have the children take turns finding the prop that they think describes God from the verse that was just read. Ask them to explain the verse using the prop. (Explain to the kids that this is *worship,* for the sole purpose of thinking about *God.* It is not a costume party!)

48. Worship with God's Promises

For no matter how many promises God has made, they are "Yes" in Christ. And so through him the "Amen" is spoken by us to the glory of God.

2 Corinthians 1:20

Materials Needed

- A "money tree" (can be purchased at party stores very inexpensively) or a tree branch
- Some Scripture verses that tell of the promises of God. Examples:

  John 3:16–17
  John 6:40
  John 6:47
  John 6:51
  John 14:3
  John 14:6
  John 14:21
  Romans 5:8
  Romans 8:10
  Romans 8:38–39
  1 Corinthians 3:16
  2 Corinthians 1:3–4
  2 Corinthians 1:9–10
  2 Corinthians 1:21–22
  2 Corinthians 5:17

- Paper and pens or pencils
- Scissors
- Yarn or ribbon

Step 1

Say, "Now let's *worship* God," or "This is our time to *worship* God."

Step 2

Change position: Move to a different position or place in the room. (Wait for quiet.)

Step 3

1. Each child is to find a promise from God in Scripture.
2. Have them write the promise on one side of the paper and then cut the paper into different fruit shapes for the tree.
3. Have the kids attach their cutouts to the tree.

This can be a worship moment for several weeks, because with each promise we get a clearer picture of who God is and how He feels about us! Examples:

John 14—promise of a home in heaven

Ephesians 6—obey parents and God promises you may live long on the earth

Matthew 28:20—"I am with you always"

49. Worship with God's Miracles

Now while he was in Jerusalem at the Passover Feast, many people saw the miraculous signs he was doing and believed in his name.

John 2:23

Materials Needed

- A "money tree" (can be purchased at party stores very inexpensively) or a tree branch
- Some Scriptures that tell of the miracles of God
- A Bible for each child
- Paper and pens or pencils
- Scissors
- Yarn or ribbon

Step 1

Say, "Now let's *worship* God," or "This is our time to *worship* God."

Step 2

Change position: Move to a different position or place in the room. (Wait for quiet.)

Step 3

1. Have the children look up one of the miracles in either the Old Testament or the New Testament.
2. Have them write down on one side of the paper what the miracle was and on the other side the characteristic of God the miracle shows.

Once again, this could be done over a few weeks, and the kids could work by themselves or in groups of two or three.

50. Worship with Prayer

> The Lord Almighty is with us.
>
> Psalm 46:11

Materials Needed

- One chair

Step 1

Say, "Now let's *worship* God," or "This is our time to *worship* God."

Step 2

Change position: Move to a different position or place in the room. (Wait for quiet.)

Step 3

1. Put a chair in the room to help the kids visualize God joining them.
2. Have each child tell Him one thing He means to them or one thing for which they want to thank Him. (They may stand in front of the chair or speak to Him from their seats—allow them to talk to God in a way they are comfortable.)
3. After there has been opportunity for each child to speak one or two times (depending on the size of the group), explain to the kids that they have just participated in prayer—that prayer is simply *talking directly to God.*

51. Worship with God's Favorite Things

I am the good shepherd; I know my sheep and my sheep know me.

John 10:14

Materials Needed

- Chalkboard, white board, or large piece of paper
- Chalk, white-board pens, or marker
- A list of God's favorite things (prepared ahead of time) that can be used to "prompt" the children if necessary

Step 1

Say, "Now let's *worship* God," or "This is our time to *worship* God."

Step 2

Change position: Move to a different position or place in the room. (Wait for quiet.)

Step 3

Ask the kids to name things they know God loves (they know because the Bible says it). For older kids, challenge them to find the verse that proves God loves a particular thing. (Examples: David was His beloved, God loves the meek, God loves the righteous, God loves obedience, God loves the world.) It is fun to see how many favorite things they can come up with!

52. Worship by Doing Service

Whatever you do, work at it with all your heart, as working for the Lord, not for men.

Colossians 3:23

Materials Needed

First Week

- No materials are needed. Explain the exercise. Ask the children to do a service for God during the week, over and above their normal activities—a special act of service that is done for God alone, not to be noticed by others. You may want to give them some ideas.

Second Week

- Pieces of paper
- Pens or pencils
- Offering basket

Step 1

Say, "Now let's *worship* God," or "This is our time to *worship* God."

Step 2

Change position: Move to a different position or place in the room. (Wait for quiet.)

Step 3

1. Have the children write what they did on a piece of paper (unsigned).
2. Pass around the offering basket and have them put the papers in it.
3. Review Colossians 3:23. Talk about offering our work as a sacrifice to God in worship and praise.

CONCLUSION

Presenting children the opportunity to know God is the highest calling a parent, grandparent, or teacher can have. Children who consistently come to the throne of Almighty God in worship are changed. Their world takes on new dimensions when we help to redirect the focus of their lives. Worshiping God helps our children clothe themselves in the armor of God, protecting them from the "roaring lion looking for someone to devour" (1 Peter 5:8).

We want our kids to be so close to God that nothing will be able to separate them from Him. "Neither death nor life, neither angels nor demons, neither the present nor the future, nor any powers, neither height nor depth, nor anything else in all creation, will be able to separate us from the love of God that is in Christ Jesus our Lord" (Rom. 8:38–39). *Nothing* will be able to separate them from God.

Worship is the glue!

This project began with an overwhelming desire to find the glue to stick children to a life of walking with God. The end of my search is more like a beginning for me. It has humbled and changed me by enabling me to taste true worship. I am exploding within, praising and thanking God for teaching me this truth and providing the privilege of having been used of Him in this task.

Now my prayer is that *you* will have a new and clearer understanding of worship. In fact, take a moment to review that definition of worship you wrote down as you began this book. I pray that you too will be changed and have a newly kindled passion to teach each and every child in your care how to truly worship God.

A worship relationship means a line of communication is miraculously opened. A life full of praise and thanksgiving will follow! A heart hungering after God's Word is born! A life overflowing with blessings, healing, strength, purity, and spiritual protection is ensured. Kids who know the truth about worshiping God will grow up strong in the Lord, loving to serve Him.

They will stick!

The one who calls you is faithful and he will do it.

1 Thessalonians 5:24

NOTES

Chapter 1: In Search of the Glue

1. "Teens and Adults Have Little Chance of Accepting Christ as Their Savior." 15 November 1999. Barna Research Online. 6 May 2002. http://www.barna.org/cgi-bin/PagePressRelease.asp?PressReleaseID=37. Used by permission.

2. Andy Butcher, "Next Generation of Teens Will Baffle Elders, Researcher Warns," Charisma News Service 3, no. 139 (9 October 2001). John Mark Ministries. 7 May 2002. http://www.pastornet.net.au/jmm/afre/afre0449.htm.

3. David J. Fant, *A. W. Tozer* (Harrisburg, Pa.: Christian Publications, 2001), 90.

4. American Academy of Child & Adolescent Psychiatry, "Teen Suicide," November 1998, http://www.aacap.org/web/aacap/publications/factsfam/suicide.htm. (22 May 2002).

Chapter 2: Worship

1. Marva J. Dawn, *Reaching Out without Dumbing Down* (Grand Rapids: Eerdmans, 1995), 76–77.

2. Ibid., 76.

3. Colin Brown, ed., *The New International Dictionary of New Testament Theology*, vol. 2 (Grand Rapids: Zondervan, 1976), 876–77.

4. James Montgomery Boice, "Genuine Worship," *Moody*, May/June 2001, 59.

5. "Worship Tops the List of Important Church-Based Experience." 19 February 2001. Barna Research Online. 27 March 2002. http://www.barna.org/cgi-bin/PagePressRelease.asp?PressReleaseID=83#Reference=E&Key=Marketing. Used by permission.

6. Jack Taylor, *Hallelujah Factor* (Mansfield, Pa.: Kingdom Publishing, 1999), 84.

7. Ibid., 91.

8. Ibid., 92–93.

9. Richard Foster, *Celebration of Discipline* (New York: Harper Row, 1978), 164.

10. Max Lucado, "Why Worship?" sermon tape, 2000.

11. Ibid.

Chapter 4: God Who?

1. Charles F. Pfeiffer and Everett F. Harrison, eds., *The Wycliffe Bible Commentary* (Chicago: Moody Press, 1968), 125.

Chapter 5: Learn the Language!

1. Jeff Japinga, ed., *Learning for Life, Christian Education and the Practice of Faith* (Grand Rapids: RCA Distribution Center, 2001).

Chapter 6: The Art of Focus

1. Leonard Sweet, *Soul Salsa* (Grand Rapids: Zondervan, 2000), 123.
2. Ibid., 124.

Chapter 7: Familiarity

1. James P. Steyer and Chelsea Clinton, *The Other Parent: The Inside Story of the Media's Affect on Our Children* (New York: Atria Books, 2002), 96–97.
2. Ibid., 100.
3. Quentin Schultze, Roy M. Anker, Lambert Zuidervaart, and John William Worst, *Dancing in the Dark: Youth, Popular Culture and the Electronic Media* (Grand Rapids: Eerdmans, 1990), 192.

Chapter 9: The Benefits of Worship

1. William J. Bennett, *The Broken Hearth* (New York: Doubleday, 2001), 13.
2. Jason L. Perry, *How Far Can You Go?* (Hopkins Park, Ill.: Oak Tree Publications and Oak Tree Ministries, 1998), 69.

Chapter 10: 52 Worship Moments

1. *The New Book of Knowledge*, volume 1A (Danbury, Conn.: Grolier Inc., 1981), 334.

Kathleen Chapman has worked with children's ministries for thirty years. She also writes, directs, produces, and teaches children's theater for schools and churches. She has written several books relating to children's theater and is a popular guest speaker at camps, retreats, MOPS, and numerous other events throughout the year. While the director of Maranatha! Music's Kid's Praise! Company, she produced and directed musical recordings for Focus on the Family. She has also appeared on the *Today* show with Maria Shriver. Chapman lives in San Clemente, California, with her husband of thirty-three years, Duane. They have three married children and one new grandbaby.